THE FOUR LAST THINGS

THE FOUR LAST THINGS

by

George William Rutler

*

CREDO HOUSE

EVANSTON • NEW YORK

Nihil obstat: Msgr. William B. Smith, S.T.D.
Censor Liborum

Imprimatur: Most Reverend Joseph T. O'Keefe
Vicar General
Archdiocese of New York

May 19, 1986

To
EUGENE V. CLARK

Quantum autem iustitiam coluerit
quantum amplexatus temperantiam fuerit
quanta prudentia praeditus
quantave animi fortitudine atque constantia fulciebatur
in ea potissimum aetate liberiore
qua praecipites et in malum suapte natura
homines proni esse consuevere
vix dici aut excogitare potest.

FOREWORD

The following chapters grew out of a series of Advent sermons first preached in a New York suburban parish over a course of evenings, and then in shorter version to workers in the Wall Street area at lunchtime. The purpose was to encourage reflection upon the deepest articles of faith.

No invention is needed for a priest to talk about Death, Judgement, Hell and Heaven since they are the stuff of tradition. Yet a measure of audacity is required to speak of an immortal purpose for earthiness in a cultural climate which thinks that deathless subjects are deadly. It is no bolder, though, than to approach the altar at Mass each day to display a death before Heaven and then to bring Heaven to earth.

The parish priest, whose duty is to preach in season and out of season, knows as well as anyone facing him

that if Chrysostom's golden tongue and Bossuet's silver
mind are not in the pulpit, Balaam's donkey always is.
The priest's first and last consolation is that donkeys,
despite themselves, have not only spoken suitable words,
but one of them even carried the actual Word slowly
through the Golden Gate.

These things are understood. I hope it is also stating
the obvious when I express my obligation to the heroic
patience of parishioners, the humble patience of peni-
tents, and the infinite patience of my guardian angel.

GWR
Rue Montparnasse
Paris

CONTENTS

INTRODUCTION

Death, Judgement, Hell and Heaven are facts in a creation which has a design, and that design is deliberate. The order in creation is so immense and pervasive that it has moral significance, since it encompasses all that affects us. Any disruption of it, by nuclear war or cancer, for example, strikes the mind as more than disordered; it is "unjust."

The human intellect is capable of understanding that there is a deep Truth behind creation which is responsible for the evident truths, that there is an active Intelligence behind any receptivity to intelligence. The intellect is really human because it has that capacity. Natural observation of this state of affairs senses from the platform of earth that this Intelligence does not simply have a will but, in some magnificent way, actually is Will.

The very fact of Will can do things. So, for instance, when Will thinks of life, life takes form. For a human to will a thing would be to start an operative chain. To say, "Let there be . . ." would begin a series of responsibilities. "Let there be light" would mean that someone is supposed to turn on a switch. But for the divine Will, the command and the chain of command are one and the same: "And God said, 'Let there be light,' and there was light." (*Gen. 1:3*) Natural intelligence naturally concludes that this Will intends a peaceful network of harmonious relationships. This intention, evident in the way all is good when things go "right," is so persistent that it can even repair calamity. There was a moment, for instance, when a leper said to Jesus of Nazareth: "If you will it, you can make me clean." Then came the reply, "I will it; be clean." (*Mark 1:40-41*) It happened as the words were spoken.

So far, at least, it should be apparent that the God of Order is not the Lord of Caprice. To do anything by chance would be a self-contradiction for him. While in a technical sense he is capable of incapacitating himself, in a moral sense to compromise his absolute Will by adding whimsey would be to annihilate all that has been made by him. In so many words, then, the basic evidence against any denial of God's existence is the fact that creation, which can be ruined, cannot be undone. Things may happen by chance, and may even be wrecked by chance, but they are not made by chance. That would be tantamount to designing an accident.

By definition, accidents are events that are not planned and never have been; except, that is, for one hideous interruption of the created order. And because that occasion was so singular it has a special name, "The Fall," and the cause of it has a name as well, "The One Against" or Satan. Any other belief in deliberate accidents is a passing superstition. That is to say, it is a most peculiar superstitiousness based on a system of associations which very many people refuse to recognize as blithe assumptions. Modern credulity rests ever so tentatively on the ultimate denial of logic, the false truism. By thinking "It goes without saying" or "As everyone knows," the modern intellect ventures to claim that the classical philosophies of certitude were invented by coincidences of molecular energy in dour ancient brains, or that the whole azure and emerald world was caused by an unmentionable gamble gambled by a gambler who never was, but whose words and shapes sort of tumbled together into piles of metrical sonnets and Persian carpets.

The blatancy of the pretense notwithstanding, facts contradict it. Perceived in their lasting significance, the frivolity of a fountain may be as titanic as a roaring cataract, for both share in a lofty scheme. And if a man could see the Intelligence that shaped one drop of either, he might die from fear or, as the saints declare is the more likely, from love. God actually did declare his intelligence, truth, and will to be the factors the sum of which has come to be called Love. The delight which Love himself takes in creation is a calculated delight in a deliberate project, and the "resting" he did on the first Sabbath would have been the wake of an unfathomable brooding which, with equal effortlessness, made the rock and the feather, the crystal and the peacock.

Creation is what it is because God is what he is. Had creation been created by the monochromatic technocrats of modernism, there would be no zebras or parrots or tigers. Their utilitarian zoos would have only one species to exhibit and it would be the Great White Shark, or on a dismal day perhaps an albino slug. But God is positively

exhuberant in his creating. Everything about him is ex-
travagant but nothing is extraneous; nothing is useless
to him because he does not confine utility. It is a mysterious economy, compact yet surpassing measure in the
same instant. Nor is it in any way uncharacteristic of
God, whose abiding nature is to make the world a loom
and a playing field and a box of gradual surprises. Quite
possibly, or at least not improbably, Jesus of Nazareth
spent free time in his carpentry shop carving secret
things. Had anyone asked what they were, he might
have tossed them back into a cabinet, locked it, and
replied: "Not much. Just some bits that light-skinned
people one day will call Chippendale."

There is an elegance to the whole operation, though
it is a terrible elegance, exacting from the Divine Creator
a cost no human can count. It was, however, shown
furtively from time to time, as when Jesus became pale
and said to the ears of a deaf man: "Be opened." (*Mark
7:34*) This was not the pallor of a salon's elegance, but
a pallor drained, and it made him groan. This at least
can be known, as Cicero resolved in the Forum when
he examined the planets way out of earshot from the
cry of a crucified Jew: there is not a shred of absentmindedness in the act of creation. It measures up to
something and its Creator is a flawless accountant:
". . . the very hairs of your head are all numbered."
(*Luke 12:7*) And even as his own tribes lost count, his
form as a young man made lame by nails towered above
them and chanted: "It is completed!"

Natural evidences of a deep Intelligence-Truth-Will
at the heart of the world may be considered in terms of
design, physical law, conscience, history, or the way one
event causes another. But these remain natural evidence. On the one hand, the students of nature, depth

psychologists and cosmologists, have attained a complexity of sophistication in their formulations which points through that nature to the impulse behind it. The plain question of *what* life is has become inextricably bound up in scientific analysis of *why* life is. On the other hand, some schools of theology have so levelled, or horizontalized, their perspective that they are producing little other than poetic physicists, and poor ones at that. The modernist impoverishment of theology is already blatantly dated, and the last generation's architects of the "secular city" are now beginning to acknowledge in halting ways that man now lives in a post-modern city where God is again sought from under the high-tech rubble.

Physics, which is the science of nature, and metaphysics, which is the science of the source of nature, are no more incompatible than a word processor and a novelist; but when they lose a sense of their respective functions they lose their integrity and their utility. The Sacred Scriptures have much to say in praise and regret of nature, but they are not satisfied to prove God's existence by it. Indeed, the Bible does not set out to prove anything about God. It is *from* God rather than *about* him and, fittingly enough, it concludes with a Revelation instead of a Conclusion. Schematic analysis and a religious critique of the secular can help pictorialize supernatural information. They can attempt some legitimate expression of the inexpressible, for in the divine order of creation, "righteousness and peace have kissed each other." (*Psalm 85:10*) But only an eternal evidence can authenticate the proofs we have from nature, and such evidence is the final key to death and what lies beyond death.

The experience of materialistic cultures shows convincingly enough that our instinct will turn in the direction of half-truths if we do not rely on supernatural guidelines for an ultimate explanation of ultimate things. These half-truths are the optimist's version of the pessimist's partial lies. Quixotic examples include the various contemporary caricatures of faithfulness, hopefulness, and loveliness which easily shrink into contempt for all three. Even after generations of false indoctrination, the mind which is intent on the eternal facts can come to realize the phenomenal misapplication of error to faith. At its roots, this false association of effect and cause is not a form of religion; it is the single alternative to it. Superstition begins when the common appetite, which like the distorted ego is an emptiness trying to fill itself, starts to make mammon a proper name. The difference between mammon and Mammon is the difference between sacramentalism and sensuality.

When mammon becomes Mammon, inflated reason fabricates lies to satisfy the soul's hunger for an explanation of its creative impulse. The audacious paganism behind this is no less erroneous when it moves into modern dress and replaces a municipal goddess with a municipal bond, a Babylonian flood epic with a Marxist social dialectic, or Venus with the venality of some pulp magazine. A cult of a supine materialism remains. It discards the transcendant reference but keeps the ritual. Crowds carry large photographs of philosophers through the streets on May Day the way they once hauled ikons. Some dress oddly in the evening and enter discotheques like stylized antique shades of souls invading deep vaults of Mithras. The whole business is so much hot air; and the meanest thing about hot air is the way it leaves men and women cold when they move outside to look at the high planets.

This may seem like "ivory tower talk" to anyone who thinks there ever were ivory towers. But even as metaphor, an ivory tower is not much. Supernaturalists are better than materialists, or Mammonists, when it comes to making good metaphors. They summon a batallion of texts and verses at their disposal to speak of Adam's fall even while the Mammonists cautiously suggest that he merely tripped. If there is one incontestable poetic about this it is the way mystics tend to be phenomenally descriptive nearly to the point of harshness, while materialists glide habitually into abstract sentimentalism. The saint will believe in a chosen people covered with desert sand and capable of crime; he could never be so weak as to share the Nazi's belief in a master race licensed to incinerate crime. The saint is quite definite about spiritual warfare in high places and the distant throb of Armageddon; he cannot possibly accept Marx's fairy tale about social classes wherein human personalities strike light against dark until the whole world is filled with singing tractor drivers and smiling ballet dancers. The contrast of Christian realism with atheistic subjectivism has consequences for the implications of created order. It boils down to the great difference between sacramentalists worshipping God nailed to a tree and naturalists behaving as though there were gods inside trees.

A Christian who understands the mystical vision is so committed to practical things that he understands, for example, that angels are neither big nor small, for they can be only great and humble. He tolerates the hard fact that pure intelligences, which is what angels are, differ in place and not in size; and while big cannot fit into small, this can fit into that. If the Mammonist pressed for some answer, the mystic could reply by saying that angels fit on pins the way they fit on galaxies, and that they delight in the lighting of a match with the same basic dance they do for an explosion on a sun. The Mammonist's quintessential atavism, since it abandons reason for a modern thing called rationalism, really declares it irrational for time and space to be ambiguous. That is, it rejects the likelihood of there being a youthfulness simultaneous with venerability, a minuteness the size of vastness, and a state in which predictions are reflections, infants outweigh emperors, embryos excel judges, and the last are first.

The rationalist makes things difficult for himself by dismissing this as irrational when it is positively a-rational. Eternity and infinity have to extend outside the scope of natural analysis by their very frame of reference. A yardstick can no more contradict infinity than a mute can expect to contradict an orator. The divine presence in the infant Jesus was at the same time older than the dinosaurs which antedated the farm animals eating the stable straw; and the nursery words babbled there came from the mouth of the Word which caused all things to be. The human mind cannot encompass this mystery, but it is obliged to assent to it; otherwise it risks confusing what is childlike with what is childish. Instead of contradicting reason, this a-rational perspective "prodicts" it, or dictates information to a reason which has no program for it. When the eternal Word in Jesus says, "I am the Beginning and the End," (*Rev. 1:8, 11; 21:6; 22:18*) the unaided reason confined to chronological time receives it as a silly non-computation, a little like a dog chasing its own tail. And when he says "Before Abraham was, I am," (*John 8:58*) the theologically unlettered accuse him of being ungrammatical.

In the grammar of intellect and will, it takes trust, or

faith, to be realistic, and only a realist can want to be faithful. The writer to the Hebrews (*11:3*) told them: "By faith we understand that the world was created by the word of God, so that what is seen is made out of things which do not appear." Faith is also exacting. Even in the elemental physical order, it does not hesitate to demand of the reader that the page he is reading is to a large degree nonmatter, that the reader himself is moving in four directions at once, and that if his body were as dense as many stars its subatomic particles would be able to fit on the head of a pin.

This is just a pedestrian route to the marvellous working by which, if incompletely decipherable, our Lord moves all things toward a purpose. Even, or perhaps especially, the miracles of his earthly ministry were signs pointing the way to a goal and not tricks proving a tenet. He operated by obedience to the eternal motive of Love as Intelligence-Truth-Will. Miracles may test human faith, but they do not tease it; faith is not credulity. It substantially confirms the intuitions of right reason because it is trust in an invisible order. And nothing can be invisible until it exists. Objects real or unreal may be unseen, but only certain, real objects are capable of invisibility. This is a point which sometimes escapes translators. For instance, "seen and unseen" is an inadequate rendering of the credal formula "visibilium et invisibilium." To be unseen is a condition of position; to be invisible is a condition of being. The best of the school men understood this; hence, St. Anselm's *fides quaerens intellectum*. This means that faith in the invisible requires knowledge and not a lack of it; we can only conceive of invisibility because there are at least some invisible things. In the moral realm this confidence in ordered reality justifies the eminently practical mystic, St. Teresa

of Avila, as she remarks her preference for intelligence
over against uninformed piety when choosing a confes-
sor: "A truly-learned man has never yet disappointed
me." Her grasp of the high invisible plan behind life
helped introduce her to ecstasy while protecting her
from mere enthusiasm.

It hardly matters that this cooperative association of
trust and knowledge might seem like a roundabout syl-
logism which runs the risk of confusing the two. Personal
experiences teach in their own ways that mazes do not
necessarily dismay; when the right exit is a possibility,
they can produce the amazement for which they were
designed. Both dismay and amazement were the reac-
tions which Jesus provoked among the people who took
him seriously. These responses are inevitable when per-
ceptions, truths, and willingness confront the seminal
Intelligence-Truth-Will displayed in utter humility. The
response is either a conspicuous wonder or disappointment. The wonder is the child of humility; the disappointment is more like the French bishop at the Orleanist
restoration who is said to have informed the assembled
nobility that Christ the Carpenter was quite well-con-
nected on his mother's side. The bishop's account of the
enfleshment of the Eternal One was a close cousin to
the more recent response which says the Messiah was
nothing but a carpenter, and an angry one at that. Christ
the Courtier, and Christ the Populist too, are close fantasies born of a disappointment with him. Since Jesus
consistently humbled those in his entourage without
humiliating them, it stands to reason that he learned the
kingly art from himself. His carpentering, instead of a
humiliation, was an intentional humbling of himself to

a human station through which he might make perfect the access of nature to the supernatural.

A life lived some thirty years in a carpenter's shop is of course going to have a carpenter's point of view, even when the view is to Heaven. Mediaeval typologists appreciated this better on the whole than we, as they deftly tongue-and-grooved the wood of the crêche with the wood of the cross. Knowing how to build houses, Christ warned against building them on sand (*Matt. 7:26-27*) and solemnly disclosed on the Galilean shore how he would build his Church on rock. (*Matt. 16:18*) No sane kind of construction, abstract or concrete, ideological or economic, should begin otherwise. To be precise, it would be crushing to begin with the roof. The principle is so obvious that it has been widely ignored, first in the designs of Renaissance humanism and then declining toward Liberal idealism, until the scene is now littered with a variety of castles in the air, none having a foundation other than subjective impressions. When you ask why they were built that way, the architects will reply that they were trying to avoid ivory towers.

The hammering of those constructions has the ring of the rejoinder frequently heard from individuals who consider themselves liberated from trust: "That may be true for you, but it is not true for me." The words dismiss the entire human experience of reasoned discourse. They would, if permitted, accomplish the tyranny of sentiment which already has crippled modern intellectual debate. The tendency of that sentiment, hardly a school and in fact more like a climate, is to take the measure of all things according to derivative intelligences about the material order; the result succumbs to a polemicism over and above logic. The freethinker shouts down visiting lecturers, the freelover de-sexes

sex, the radical feminist turns *ad hominem*, the existentialist declares his heroes immortal, and so on. It is fascist
in that it pays tribute to the strength of movements
rather than to the substance of truth. The cost of it
bankrupts basic freedom because freedom needs a solid
standard, and not an airy assumption, as its guarantee.
The secularizer does not take Heaven and Hell seriously
because he has not learned to take earth very seriously.
His abuse of the integral personality may so obliterate
his perception of historical being that he first loses grip
on the conscience and then on the will. When that happens, the same mentality which spoke of eschatology, or
knowledge of ends, narrows itself to a confined discussion of natural ecology.

Cynics, who are to sentimentalism what sadists are to
sense, whisper into the secular ear singularly disordered
information about the balance of the world; they may
say that there is indeed a beach and it is our beach, but
there is not nor ever was a sea, and that the only basis
for life is its bottom. To take one example, this bereft
cynicism accounts for the subjectivist's refusal to believe
how Jesus walked on water. The apostolic belief in such
an event demands a harder look at water than the subjectivist can manage and, quite more threateningly, it
requires a freedom to follow the miracle-worker when
he walks on the shore. Christ treading heavily on the
water is of moral interest; Christ stepping lightly on solid
ground is of cosmic magnitude. That is why Peter's body
sank when the Rabbi from Heaven asked him to walk
on water, and why his heart sank when the Rabbi made
him a rock: "On this rock I will build my church." (*Matt
16:18*)

The secularizer's impressionism would be less harmful
to self-understanding were it only a kind of naiveté, like

Comte's Positivism with its "Religion of Humanity."
Then at least some remnant of common sense might be
able to condense the perception of reality before it fades
into the mist of utopianism. But it does in fact do a lot
of damage as it obscures the divine Will at work in the
created order. The first victim of the cerebral wound
is the rational appreciation of historical progress. "As
the rationalist had destroyed faith in Reason," wrote
Christopher Dawson in *Progress and Religion*, "so it was
the work of the historian to undermine man's belief in
the unity of history." He gives three explanations for
the subterfuge: the modern obsession with the State as
the primary ordering principle of human conduct, thus
obliterating the Church's respect for the principle of
subsidiarity; the fragmented attentions of scientific history which "departmentalize" experience; and the disregard of anthropologists for the valuable role played
by the historic consciousness in giving a sense of proportion to the social sciences.

Historical unity, as evidence of a divine plan about
which the science of ultimate things, or eschatology,
speaks, is not the sort of mechanical arrangement which
the old-line Deists of the rationalist generations attrib-
uted to an Architect-God. These Deists crippled the hu-
manizing perspective of historical development. Once
that happened, historians began to think of ends instead
of an End. The historical line of the Deists was simply
circumstance set in motion; the procession of history
filtered through the mind as an inevitable and, indeed,
unstoppable progression in which moving ahead had to
mean getting better. You could almost hear the capital
"P" in the progressivist's breath as he began to speak,
not of progress as a moral consequence, but of Progress
as a palpable and autonomous reality. Spencer rallied

the faint Victorian skeptics: "Progress is not, therefore, an accident but a necessity . . ." No longer would progress march, but it would be a march of its own: to speak of "The March of Progress" signifies nothing more than "The Progress of Progress," but the phrase sounds noble enough to enlist whole generations of well-meaning yet half-awake people in its course.

The idea of Progress had come to be an exhilarating substitute for distant and uninspiring gods. But since grace perfects nature, grace is not static, and the God of grace is at once both remote and immanent. The rationalist God was only remote, a regulating watchmaker but not a creating carpenter. One measures, the other builds: "Destroy this temple and in three days I will build it . . ." (*Mark 14:58*) Either this claim of Scripture is prophecy or bravado, and the deistic sensibility was sorely put to the test while it tried to decide. A decision was required, as it is now; just as one cannot evade an issue by simply agreeing the man was sane though he mistakenly believed himself to be Napoleon, or that Popes are wise and distinguished humanitarians who have been wrongly persuaded that they can be infallible. If a wise man is not mistaken about so serious a matter, it is plain that Christ, both wise and good, was not mistaken about rebuilding the Temple. The question is really more serious: how was he able to do it.

The props Christ used to rebuild the Temple were elementary, being two wooden beams and three iron nails; and the Temple was personal, for it was his own body, not as a metaphysical conceit but rather as a blatantly literal fulfillment of the Semitic belief that the holy could be housed. It is very important to realize that the rebuilding was a resurrection; that is to say, it was more than a redundant reconstruction. It is a change, and an improvement, and a building up of the personal Temple. Spiders rebuild their old webs in the same way because they have limited intelligence and no reason, but Christ brought perfect intelligence and reason into the created order. So the old Temple, which was an intimation of perfect order, had to be reformed in a new way to become the perfect order itself.

The result was that the resurrection of Christ, understood as the apparition of the living Temple of God, became a perfection of history, which was now redirected upwards to its transcendent origin after it had been so long falling down. When he rose from the dead, genealogy was given a new frame deliberately called his body, or his church, which is the same thing: "Now therefore you are no more strangers and foreigners, but fellow citizens with the saints, and of the household of God; and are built upon the foundation of the apostles and prophets, Jesus Christ himself being the chief corner stone; in whom all the building fitly framed together grows into a holy temple in the Lord in whom you also are built together for a habitation of God through the Spirit." (*Eph. 2:19-22*) The language is shamelessly fundamentalistic; shamelessly so, that is, because it is perfectly proper and even necessary to be a fundamentalist, but only about fundamentals.

The architectural mistake of starting with the roof instead of the floor symbolizes the attempt at a faith that has no authentic tradition. The temporary appeal of such tenuous religiosity is understandable. It is normal for the human disposition to seek quick warmth when acquaintances turn chill, and to want protection when the fray becomes intense. But the practicality of history proves, as we said before, that a house with a roof floating above and no foundation beneath is a dream castle.

Such fantastic habitations have become almost as numerous as ivory towers are few. As dreamers learn, such
houses vanish the second the alarm clock, or the shock
of mortality, breaks the black loveliness of the night.

That shock of awakening is striking Catholics today
with the realization that many earnest attempts to provide an authentic reason for belief in a cynical age have
done quite the opposite. They have only managed to
uproot the foundation of experience and substitute credulity for realism. Once victimized by that credulity, the
degenerating intellect starts to suppose that probably
nothing, nothing at all, follows upon the traces of death.
The chipped cornerstone of high hope and altruism is
still there, but it is washed about by a flood of watery
materialism, ignorance of doctrine, and an accompa-
nying pedantry. More authorities can explain who did
not write parts of the Bible than can preach what those
parts mean. The result can be positively ironic: while
liturgists pursue a half-fabricated ideal called Primitiv-
ism, anthropologists create a new science called Futur-
ism; and while the dogmatician decides that it is safer
to concentrate on what is called the "ground of being,"
the cosmologist searches outer space for "curved time."
The reductionist or neo-modern trend in religious
thought quickly finds itself labelled "out of date" by the
same Spirit of the Age which it tried to date, but which
is then promptly spurned in its turn. The modernist
rehabilitated himself in a neo-modern outfit only to find
that the world had become post-modernist. The beguiling Spirit of the Age was only and ever a reflection,
seeing the human drama backwards instead of inwards.

Reflection is the recourse of the soul which has lost

the gift of contemplation. The thinking done by the reductionist is enormously self-centered; it can hardly be otherwise when the object of study is a mirror. Self-centeredness arrests moral development, for no healthy growth is possible without a tradition which gives continuity to change. From a mature point of view, change without continuity is a perpetual adolescence; such is what makes change at times a mutation. The propensity to breathless egoism, so characteristic of the reductionist design in philosophical constructions, certainly has its antecedents, as it provoked Saint Paul: "Brothers, I myself was unable to speak to you as people of the Spirit; I treated you as sensual men, still infants in Christ. I fed you with milk, not solid food, for you were not ready for it." (*I Cor. 3:1*) Like the other Pauline metaphor of the foundation, this food finds its integrity in substantiality.

Various listeners remarked that the confidence with which our Lord spoke was different from that of the scribes who kept circling around truths. They meant that he not only described true things, but more than circumscribing them, he seemed to be a house for them. If it is not too irreverent to say, the integrity of Christ's rabbinicism was in the style of Trollope's Mrs. Stanhope, who decorated her constructions and did not condescend to construct a decoration. Or it was something like actually seeing a single number when looking at numerous things, a feat no one has ever accomplished. We do the latter when we try to figure out the Trinity; but Three-in-One cannot be counted, it has to be seen, and that we cannot do while we remain on earth.

There were times when our Lord abandoned figures and became speech. These were the times he showed the four last things around which we have constructed our various confidences and fears, and to which every ideal and work of art is some form of tribute. Certainly without acknowledging these four ends, the Catholic believer is neither Catholic nor believing; for these are the basic utterances about which all else is commentary, and so they compose the foundation of all salutes and confessions. To be a Catholic, to be a Christian, let us say to be human, one has to consider how to die a holy Death, how to pass Judgement, how to avoid Hell, and how to attain Heaven.

They proclaim themselves the Four Last Things, the *eschata*, and are properly that since they are not only the things that come last but the things that do last. The transformation of the word "last" from an adjective and adverb to a verb is a deft and cosmic sleight of hand. Even when one is not looking, it can make the difference between life and death itself. When one is looking as one should, the change will guide the recognition by which the aided intellect learns to contain that joy promised by Jesus, who vowed that the stones would cry out and call him the Christ, the Son of the Living God.

Should we be disposed to think that nothing lasts, we would still not be freed from the Four Last Things themselves, for they do perdure. This age, which has succumbed to the temptation to think itself the first to have "come of age," will be let in on their secret one way or another. It may happen in a passing moment, when the age suddenly feels unsatisfied with affluence gained by compromise, or after a long struggle to distance itself from trust in the existence of a moral universe. The secret of the Four Last Things will come as a surprise whether the age turns to the West or to the East. The secret is as public as the world and as obvious as its circumference. The astonishment will shower life with the one sensation which the bullies of sentiment and the engineers of instability could never provide in all their experiments and days, and that is joy full of joy.

ONE

THE POINT OF DEATH

And when Jesus had crossed again in the boat to the other side, a great crowd gathered about him; and he was beside the sea. Then came one of the rulers of the synagogue, Jairus by name; and seeing him, he fell at his feet, and besought him, saying, "My little daughter is at the point of death. Come and lay your hands on her, so that she may be made well, and live." And he went with him. (*Mark 5:21-24*)

The mind is capable of distinguishing between life and existence. It is believed that "where there is life there is hope," and it follows that where there is eternal life there is eternal hope. Yet no normal person is particularly eager to die in order to attain eternity. The desire for life is so inclusive that existence is most tolerable only when life yields to some kind of superlife: "For while we are still in this tent, we sigh with anxiety; not that we would be unclothed, but that we would be further clothed, so that what is mortal may be swallowed up by life." (*2 Cor. 5:4*)

Since earthly life is brief, St. Paul's statement might almost be considered a fleeting thought. But the oppressiveness of mortality can become a source of lifelong anxiety when it is not faced head on. To be realistic about this is sheer common sense, but sensible people do not like anything to be common; they especially do not like to be sensible, hence the crippling divorce between sensibility and sense. The easy thing to do, then, is to become distracted from life's "fleeting shadow" by the sheer bulk of what appear to be longer lasting things like buildings and books. Architects and writers are more easily tempted to pompous statements about life and death than farmers and seamen, whose livelihood demands that they respect the impetuousness of the world of land and water in which they live. True artfulness is more likely to begin when an architect stops making statements and starts making houses, just as an author starts being profound when he surmounts the temptation to write for the ages and learns how to write for the aging. Otherwise, creativity has a tendency to crumble into a self-conscious imitation of creation when it should participate in it.

To be authentic, any kind of enterprise needs some link to history and family, and not merely to opinion. Without that continuity, the assumption of authority is an arbitrary arrogation. There is a world of difference, for instance, between assuming a throne and assuming a solution; the royal "we" has often been brave, while the editorial "we" has more often been bravado. Kings are history and most did not feel obliged, as many of their troublesome ministers did, to make history. Events happen, but history does not. To make history is something like making a bed; one can really only arrange it, and it will be there no matter what is done to it. So, then, the objection to monarchy is the best reason for it; a king has no special qualifications and in that sense he alone can be history. "Any ruler can rule," said St. John Chrysostom, "but only a king can die for his people."

Great achievers *do* things for multitudes; the central function of a king is to be un*done* for them. In a kingdom of subjects striving for immortality, the king's crowning glory is his mortality. No confident king would take seriously phrases like "the parade of time" and "passing on the torch of freedom" and "belonging to the ages," although officious people use them all the time because importance seems to be a thing which can be got by becoming part of some recollection. In many court annals, the intense prime minister could barely conceal his contempt for the king's ballroom-promenading and horse-marching, while he labored in his shuttered bureau choreographing the Parade of Time. Time is no more capable of parading than is the atmosphere, but the grand rhetoric lets a certain frame of mind think that it can continue to live by being kept, as they say, "alive" in someone else's memory. If to die is to leave history, the alternative to leaving history is to become historic. This is the bureaucratic version of immortality.

When other things are forgotten, the date of birth and date of death remain chiselled in stone. From the standpoint of curiosity, these are the dullest bits of information that can be inflicted on others. "Vital statistics" are about as revealing as calling the Norman Conquest an event that occurred in 1066. But even if time does not "parade" or history "march," people do; and there are points at which they start and end.

Such consciousness flows in torrents through the

Scriptures. Esau says to Jacob, "I am at the point of death, of what use is my birthright?" (*Gen. 25:32*) A court official asks Jesus to heal his son "for he was at the point of death." (*John 4:47*) Jairus of the synagogue pleads to him, "My little daughter is at the point of death. Come and lay your hands on her that she may be made well, and live." (*Mark 5:23*) The ones "at the point" in these cases were young people. Now when a chef says that a particular dish is cooked *à point*, he is showing off his skill; but while we may or may not be ready for it, death itself can happen without anyone getting it ready. The death of young people is the ruddy stuff of tragedy because it seems to be so out of line and unskilled. Moses falling in a heap on ancient stones is one thing, young Shelley stretched out like a damp sponge is quite another. But both were equally dead. The very phrase "an untimely death" is about as fatuous as an untimely life. There is a big difference between saying "time is up" and "it's time," but that does not prevent us from reaching a point at which they mean the same. When St. Paul said he was as one born out of time, he meant that it was about time he was born.

The death of the young, a grief to parents and a poignancy to all who are conscious of a vanished potential, is also cold proof that death requires no experience. Babies die as efficiently as old people. It almost seems in a dreadful way that, just as the better swimmer uses fewer strokes, the very young are better at dying free of fuss than their elders. Death is one of life's two points, and there is no reason why it should require more training than the first point. Babies still manage to be born without the benefit of clinical instruction, so it should not seem odd that anyone can die without taking a course in it.

By the same token, the human race has sat through enough Socratic soliloquies and Italian operas to know that one can also die with flair and at length. Daniel Webster's deathbed addresses make up a volume. But it states the obvious to say, regardless of the amount of battle smoke and hymnody surrounding it, that death as an incident has the same effect regardless of attendant circumstance. There are tales of strong men choking on cherries, and of the soldier surviving the Battle of the Bulge only to swallow a bee in his beer. The fittest physiques can die from a few missed dinners. And, as important, it eventually happens one way or another to everyone. The poet can rage against the dying of the light, but that just makes it noisy.

Then there is the Englishman who upon reading an account of Aeschylus and his strange death, took out an insurance policy, at favorable odds, against the fatal chance of an eagle dropping a tortoise shell on his own head. There is less certainty now about the odds in another matter: namely, having an unfriendly power drop an atomic bomb on your head. One would not dismiss the anxiety about the horrid nuclear threat even when the pacifist's approach to that menacing frontier indicates a transparent decline of confidence in rationalism. An overwrought rationalism disingenuously externalizes the interior struggle between good and evil; utopian pascifism has to be purely evasive if it comes to suggest that total disarmament will in any way reduce the odds of our dying. In Adam all die, the emphasis being on all as much as on Adam, and the tortoise shell was as fatal to Aeschylus as a missile might be to people on the street in Moscow or New York. That more can die from the latter does not mitigate the statistic which shows that the universal death rate is still one hundred per cent, regardless of weaponry.

At least one development has affected modern attitudes on death: the way we are now able to isolate ourselves from the ordinary sight of people dying. The world is losing an entire literary genre in the process; it is harder to make significant deathbed orations from intensive-care units than from four-posted canopied beds. By this probably comes a loss to culture second only to that of letter-writing as a consequence of the telephone. So one is inclined not to notice how most people at the point of death deal with it in a rather natural, quiet and even graceful way. Evidently the fear of death is as nothing compared to the fear of life. There is more crying in a delivery room than from a death bed. The baby cries while onlookers smile; at a death, the opposite is the more frequent case. David's lament for Absalom has never stopped.

Death is commonly more difficult for the survivors, because sorrow is love without its object. Some mourners, very frequently bereaved children among them, go through a period of anger at the dead for having died. Others have nothing to say, as if silence might erase an absence just as speech opens a wound. The unspeakable pain is as old as the oriental lament; for if history does not march, it certainly can seem to drag, and behind its back is a most heavy weight. "Infandum Regina jubes renovare dolorem." Aeneas placed the dark burden at the feet of Dido: "O Queen, you bid the retelling of a grief that should never be uttered".

In less metric fashion, and for less human reason, such sorrow has become one of the few things left that can shock a sullen humanity. The progress of modern totalitarianism illustrates how sexual license is soon followed by a morbid license which makes pain a fetish. Nudity in the films, for instance, soon yields to "explicit violence." The sequence is not odd; it is the pattern of Eden. Cain struck Abel as the next tumble in the fall of naked Adam. Purity is strength and impurity leads to a fatal weakness which tries to dissipate its own sorrow by inflicting it on others. Ancient people cut themselves in grief; modern people cut others. Cruelty is a measure of how bereft we feel, and the increased brutality in the discontented social order is a gauge of the inability to fathom the meaning of death.

The facts of death are withheld from children the way the facts of life used to be. Of course it is an insincere modesty, as is clear in the macabre fascination which ritually accompanies the funerals of Hollywood stars and more distinguished public figures. As God would not tolerate fig leaves or death in paradise, so a decline in the human consciousness of God perverts the proper regard for both. When the return to paradise seems blocked, the lingering scent of its gardens becomes a grief. Outside paradise everything is forbidden but the fruit and various sorts of deficiencies set in, as they would for anyone who tried to live on an unbalanced diet. In the speculative order the chief deficiency is the inability to know what bodies are. This is a basic corollary of the refusal to hear news of what God is. The timid theist, in the manner of the first man and woman, has his own pornography and, true to its word, it has to do with a show of the flesh. The atheist, however, has nothing to do with that. Death is the only pornography of atheism. In the atheist's version of the fairy tale, the source of scandal would not be a Naked Emperor but a Dead Emperor.

We might note that death is only a problem for humans. Beasts, with a limited intelligence and a vacant will, resist killers; but only humans, with a creative rea-

son and a free will, can contemplate the enormity of
what that killer is doing. The object of the animal's fear
is not death but any sudden, painful interruption of
death's natural course. Lacking an imaginative intellect,
the animal has no wide reference; it sees frame by frame
but does not see the whole motion picture.

Contemplation is the endowment of a soul, which only
humans have. Composed as it is of vital reason and will,
the soul can engage in activities which are not material.
Aristotle contemplating the bust of Homer is of course
a double contemplation, for Rembrandt pictured Aristotle doing it. Nothing contemplates in hives, for all their
buzzing; and nothing contemplates in herds, for all their
lumbering. Humans do it in town and country in every
circumstance. The human ability to discover physical
truths, done so adroitly in the latest theories of relativity
and quantum mechanics and antimatter, is less wonderful than the ability to be aware of the ability itself.
Einstein said that the most incomprehensible thing
about the universe is that it is comprehensible. Part of
that comprehension is the capacity to give it value; indeed, it is the higher part, for it is less important to
speak of matter and anti-matter than to conclude that
they do matter.

The soul, understood as a spiritual element in which
the conscience and will thrive and properly function
according to reason, engages in these immaterial acts
because it is an individual reality. General intelligence
does not require a personality behind it, but reason does;
and this fact, regardless of the pessimism of the atheist,
is precisely why the immaterial matters to us. As the
Congregation for the Doctrine of the Faith expresses it

(May 7, 1979), it is by means of this endowment of the soul that the human "I" subsists.

When a grown man or woman becomes sophisticated enough, as do some children and all saints, to believe in the existence of angels, he or she may then come to learn that angels are pure intelligence but have no reason, their intelligence being purely intuitive. Their characters do not require the individuating capacity for experimentation and conclusion which is the talent of human personality. Satan, being a fallen angel, can only operate through imitation and the destruction of what has already been created. Humans function intelligently through bodies, under the governing principle of reason, and in this sense they are able to create and order affairs as neither angels in the higher order are meant to do nor animals in the lower order can.

When God became human in Jesus, divine intelligence assumed the operation of human reason. The unique cohesion gave us the one case of a perfect personality. Christ mimicked no one and no one could mimic him. The event of Christ is far more important, therefore, as history than as philosophy. Theories about him refer back to him; he does not follow upon theories about him. The accounts of his life were not fabricated or altered to accommodate the prophecies about him. The prophecies are kept as prophecies today only because they agreed with him, and not because he was *made* to agree to them. In the most explicit language, Jesus is not a mere symbol to prove a point; he is, as no one else has been able to be, the point of symbolism.

The practical inseparability of the soul and the body in the definition of a human was an historic change which St. Thomas Aquinas highlighted in his appropriation of Aristotelian language. It was a dramatic

movement beyond Aristotle, who could not conceive
how the body might function spiritually as the visible
form of the soul which is in turn the substantial form
of the body. As a link between the material and the
immaterial, the gift of reason is a spiritual endowment
which operates through the carnal state by divine intent.
The operation of reason is a complementary economy,
as contemplation of life requires generation of life. Here
is where hope finds a home, for if sorrow is love without
its object, joy is love in active contemplation of its object,
and such contemplation is the activity of reason. Hope,
in union with happiness, is rational. When hope is based
on a love, which is a union with God who is the source
of happiness, it is more than an emotional exercise and
far more than a sentimental diversion. It is the proper
result of right reason contemplating the right object.
This is why St. Augustine wrote his much misunderstood
injunction, "Love God and do as you please." If we love
properly, we are properly rational, and we are that only
if our pleasure pleases God. Otherwise, reason denies
itself and becomes a self-defeating rationalism which is
the antithesis of hope and the evasion of love. When
reason is lost, we have to rationalize. We go back then
to the hive and herd; and when the mourner is asked
what is the lost object of his love, he can only reply with
Buckminster Fuller's definition of any human: "A self-
balancing 28-jointed adaptor-based biped, an electro-
chemical reduction plant integral with segregated stow-
ages of special energy extracts."

The Eighteenth Century, which is erroneously called
the Age of Reason when it was more accurately an age
of rationalizing, defined the object of its humanism the
same way, and so it lost a sense of its own soul. With this
loss began the modern plummeting into introspection

as an end in itself. Each attempt to resolve the nature
of desire produced an irresolution. The Eighteenth Century's more passionate thinkers, however, saw through
the dilemma. To be fair, the age of the skeptical Diderot
and Gibbon was more typically the age of the faithful
Dryden, Wesley, Pope and Johnson, even when the
hatchet sounds of the Terror were more commanding
than the calliopes of the Peaceable Kingdom.

Post-modern man is now able to look back and attempt
to recover a reasonable understanding of how body and
soul work together. The body is hardly a skin balloon
around the air of the soul; we know that from the virtues
and sins of the human condition. No more is the soul
couched in the more poetic part of the body around the
heart. That combination of bad anthropology and theology could only be taken seriously by some of the Sun-
day sentimentalists who are the counterpart to weekday
rationalists. Catholicism objects to this dualist heresy,
and it is a heresy, because it lacks sufficient restraint to
reason how the soul can be everywhere in an individual
and in no particular place at the same time. The soul
cannot be seen and yet it flares the nostrils in anger,
furrows the brow in deliberation, curls the lips in laugh-
ter and brightens the eyes in delight. And it turns the
flesh to stone when it leaves.

There are things like temper which become most real
to us only when we lose them. So we might plumb the
mystery of the soul by considering where it goes when
it goes "away." When the disciples asked Jesus where he
lived, he said "Come and see," even though he had no
place to lay his head. It is not unlike the case of the soul,
for when it goes "away" it goes the only way there is,

even though to us it may seem like no place in particular. Asking where the soul goes when it "passes away" is like asking where time goes when it "flies." It goes wherever it "is" and in our frustration we should not give up and try to kill time. That would cause the second worst boredom, the worst being the wake after willfulness has killed the soul.

Nothing illustrates this destruction of the soul more indictingly than the trend toward selfishness as a functioning creed. It may be given the bright title "humanism," but it nevertheless operates as a cavernous religion, absolutely Gnostic in its elite obscurantism. The humanist may give his life for the good of mankind while seeing little significance in the good of a man. John Dewey took considerable pride in the religious potential of humanism and urged, as though preaching a crusade, that it become "explicit and militant." Others content themselves with its sectarian expression in transactional analysis and encounter groups.

This is the big attempt at an autonomous and congratulatory selfishness which denies the soul as the image of God. Individuals are looked upon as lesser gods on a bleak field of inherited experience, each battling in an Hegelian exchange until some end up masters and the rest slaves. For when the cheerful American democrat begins to make "I'm O.K. You're O.K." a statement of henotheistic faith, he really strikes the first blast of that hunting call trumpeted wherever the soul is thought to be unreal: "I am out to get you." It does not take very long in the perspective of what we know to be the length of civilizations for the hunting sound, once heard only between blatant villains, to mellow into a chant sung mellifluously by the strong to the infirm, the young to the old, and even by mothers to the children in their wombs. The sound has even gone out to the courts, to decide when it is permissible for parents to kill their children. This kind of humanist cry is a Siren sound in a dark recess of human self-will, and though it may be draped in chintz and strung with the sophist's lights, it remains a darkness in which the humane jail the human.

As evidence of the inevitable cycle of counter-reaction to exaggerated reaction, a new concern for the dying has begun to distract the humanist's fear of death. The development, now called thanatology, has in its best moments fostered the hospice movement as an alternative to the clinical indignities which often accompany terminal illness; but it also may conceal its own interior bewilderment in the face of mortality. This happens when the emphasis is on adjusting to death with a moderate brand of Stoicism. A credal relativism breeds here, losing sight of the resurrection which makes the Christian appreciation of life and death unique. Studying death is like studying the piano; it can involve both the examination of an instrument and the practice of its music. The humanist's analysis is not the study of death at all but rather a study of deaths. It is adequate for taking death into account as a physical phenomenon with its psychological effects; but in relation to the cosmic significance of death, it is as limited as philology when it moves from grammar to the epic.

Above all, the empirical study of death finds both its limit and its challenge in Jesus Christ, who never counselled anyone to adjust to death. Instead, from the first indication at the Jordan river to the last shout in Jerusalem, it is evident that Jesus wants us to do death, get it over with, and then move on. There is a point of death, and Christianity refutes every suggestion that it is an illusion; not even Bostonian transcendentalism has

drowned out the solemn rumbling of the correct intuition. Salmon coursing upstream are mute testimony to
the inevitable process and the last pleiosaurus paid it
unwitting tribute; and they do not ever appear poised
with such dignity as at their funereal moment. But there
is still something deeper about it in the human intellect
than a wild intuition.

The dignity of the dying animal comes from its natural
surrender to cyclical decay. There walks through the
land another form of life which is not content to think
that the brightest promise of a corpse is its potential for
fertilizing. While there is a point of death, men and
women know that there is also a point *to* death; and it
is not merely the natural pattern of decay and regeneration. Light becomes grass; grass become cow; cow
becomes a man who likes his steak. That does not make
the man a cow; but it does give reason to say that, to
some degree, "all flesh is grass." To another degree, it
helps explain why humans become wistful when lights
fade and suns set, as if they are meant to be part of a
light that does not go out. If man is grass, then he is
obliged to return the compliment light paid grass by
entering into it. To man flushed on beef and ale did
Christ the Morning Star offer to show "the eternal
brightness of the Father's face." But this was on his own
intimate terms, so that instead of looking at it, man was
invited to "enter into" the joy of the Lord.

This call to every soul makes the human notion of
dying much different from the sombre reclinings of ex-
hausted beasts and, since it sometimes flaunts valor and
rage, less sensible and dignified. In a way that is totally
inexplicable to the biological determinist, the most sensible people—that is to say, those who are normally re-
tiring and free of exhibitionism—would die as martyrs

for some cause or on a venerable battlefield, rather than expire from botulism or on a highway. No society, however agnostically utopian, gives medals to accident victims or erects statues to tourists who eat bad shellfish. Yet there is a common international regard for an eclectic assortment who act beyond determinism: a gaunt nun who rescues infants from Calcutta streets, or John Jacob Astor calling to his wife from the deck of the Titanic, "Goodnight, my darling. I'll see you in the morning."

Both mystic and cynic alike will agree on one thing, which very simply is that death must not seem senseless if we are to make any sense of it. Even the nihilist, who thinks that only absurdity is serious, is willing to call death the ultimate absurdity. In an odd way, then, those for whom death is most insignificant are the most morbid. The saying remains true, that the skeptic believes in nothing more than death and the believer believes in nothing less than death. The release from skepticism, so long as it does not fling us into the arms of another credulity, is the only recourse to the one authentic humanism. Anything else will overrate dying and underrate death.

It is only because the skeptical Saul had been knocked off his horse on the Damascus road that the pastoral letters he left us do not mingle preachiness with their rabbinical intensity and syntax, quite unlike the way modern man stoccatos his commencement addresses and rock ballads. A believer is ordained to preach; a skeptic more often than not has to be restrained from preaching. Once a man has decided that there probably is not much worth saying, he cannot stop telling others. In the Church this skepticism takes the form of liturgy as self-expression. One clue is when church banners

decorated with uplifting aphorisms replace statues and
ikons in a ridiculously suburban Orwellianism. But the
Damascus road conversion enflamed St. Paul with a zeal
for converting others instead of improving them. His
inspired language became among the most mature ever
composed:

> I tell you this, brethren: flesh and blood cannot inherit
> the kingdom of God, nor does the perishable inherit
> the imperishable. Lo! I tell you a mystery. We shall
> not all sleep, but we shall all be changed, in a moment,
> in the twinkling of an eye, at the last trumpet. For the
> trumpet will sound, and the dead will be raised im-
> perishable, and we shall be changed. For this perish-
> able nature must put on the imperishable, and this
> mortal nature must put on immortality. (I Cor. 15:50-
> 54)

The wrong counsel would turn this into a simplistic
division of body and soul, the kind of dualism that makes
our bodies temporary cages for a spirit straining to be
free. But St. Paul says two things contrary to that facile
mistake: first, that our temporal nature can become im-
perishable by some kind of investiture; and second, that
our mortality can do the same. This is not a lyrical par-
allelism after the manner of the Hebrew psalms. The
nature and mortality of which St. Paul sings are different. They are different in that they are precisely the
body and soul which dualism thought incompatible and
which became the dark ache of Attic tragedy. The difference, or investiture, explains why the alabaster Apollo
of the Belvedere gazes from his pedestal ever more wist-
fully than the fevered Christ from the cross; and the
difference is found again in the abyss between an intrinsic circumstance which freezes the spirit into a vague
inability to die, and an extrinsic resurrection which frees

that spirit from an inability to live. For immortality is
not assured by our nature alone; there is between the
pagan and Scriptural accounts of immortality a distinction not unlike that which separates a man who cannot
sink from a man who cannot swim. The Judaeo-Chris-
tian immortality, so developed in Pharisaic thought that
St. Paul used it to divide sides at his hearing in Jerusalem, (*Acts 23:6-10*) is bestowed, or "put on," by the
divine power which created us in the first place without
our conscious cooperation. But this will be an investiture, and if it does not resurrect to eternal life, it will
resurrect us to eternal separation from life. (*Jn. 5:9;
Matt. 25:46*) So while the speaker may not describe an
inevitable mortality, he can indeed speak of an inevitable
resurrection, the only question being whether it will kill
death or life.

One of the many perils in contemplating eternal states
is the temptation to a pious vagueness; it is easier to talk
about unseen nature than invisible supernature. The
bodily assumption of the Blessed Virgin Mary, as but
one example, must strike even some believers as a dra-
conian intrusion into the ethereal. Among nonsacra-
mental Christians, it may seem an audaciously casual
account of the interaction between corporeality and
timelessness. For the dualists of any age, whose burden
is the *idée fixe* that heaven is too tasteful to transform
blatant bones, the dogma of the Assumption is like
throwing a pie in God's face. Sacred tradition says that
Mary was bodily assumed into heaven by virtue of her
having been conceived free of the curse of carnal death,
but to the dualists, this is as irrelevant as excusing the
pie thrower on the grounds that the pie was a meringue.

The Fourth Lateran Council in 1215 admonished the
Cathari sectarians for that schizophrenic view of the

divine order, which modernity has not only duplicated, but has reduced to even more literal equations. This goes to show how a large part of modern alienation is an unconscious traditionalism, albeit that the tradition is one of mistakes. Were the secular humanist as favorably disposed to humans as he is to humanity, he would not find the Council's assertion so unreasonable when it says, "All will rise with the same body that they carry below . . ." (DS 801). Only trust, in its capacity as polisher of the imagination, can open the contemplation to an appreciation of what "sameness" means for a body which is capable of being both baby and centenarian. St. Paul exhibits it when he recognizes that there is a considerable difference between saying that we shall all be reshaped and that we shall all be changed. The former is distortion while the latter is growth.

Do I stop being me when my eyes dim and when my hair goes? Or do I stop being me when I lose an arm, or does it take the loss of both arms to stop being me? Shall we bid higher? Some adults think some fetuses are not themselves because they lack certain bits; and some adolescents think the same of the elderly. Anthony of Egypt was still Anthony of Egypt when he became 105, but he had also become a whole saint. It took more than a vested interest in senility to inspire old Irenaeus to write: "When the chalice we mix and the bread we bake receive the word of God, the eucharistic elements become the body and blood of Christ, by which our bodies live and grow. How then can it be said that flesh belonging to the Lord's own body and nourished by his body and blood is incapable of receiving eternal life?" The important thing is that our body in eternity will not be somebody or anybody, but our body; and when friends see us it will not be as at a class reunion when we compare grey hair and match weight; in that higher reunion George does not match his armour to Joan's, nor do Patrick and Benedict compare tonsures; and no one will shake hands at first because the initial reaction will be to venerate, even worship, each other. And all this because first we had died.

Christ parted company with the literalist Sadducean party and its rejection of resurrection as non-Scriptural. But neither was he an orthodox Pharisee for whom, in their basic goodness, resurrection was some happy ending to the Passover experience. Christian resurrection is the Passover itself: "Christ our Passover has been sacrificed. Let us, therefore, keep the feast . . ." (*I Cor. 5:7-8*) Because the body is, in Pauline language, a tent of the soul as it helps us travel, it is not a tomb; but it is very much a sign of exile (*II Cor. 5:6*) until it "puts on Christ" through a life of continual Eucharist.

Christ's drive to get to Jerusalem, and his refusal to be deterred by those around him, was not impatience; it was, if anything, a patient humility by which the Son conformed to his Father's plan to place resurrection at the center of actual progress. To say, "I believe in God," must also mean, "I believe in life after death." All the articles of the creed are the first one said in different ways. St. Paul said that if the resurrection is a fantasy, then so all trust is a misery. If the rabbi who said, "I am the Resurrection and the Life," (*John 11:25*) was wrong, he cannot linger in admiring eyes like a valiant Jewish Ghandi. He cancels himself out. Ghandi would still have been Ghandi had there not been an independent India, but he would not have been Ghandi had there not been an India. There can be no Christ of history without a Passover in his past, and there can be no Christ beyond history without a Resurrection raising his head. So, when

the "Resurrection of Life" set about giving us resurrection and life, he went to be sacrificed at Passover "dumb
before his shearer" *(Acts 8:32;* see also *Isa. 53:7)* and
"steadfastly set his face to go to Jerusalem." *(Luke 5:51)*
It was not heroism; it was providence. Had he aimed for
some Olympus and failed, his dumbness, quite bluntly,
would have been stupidity; because he aimed for Jerusalem and succeeded, we shall find at the heart of
eternity not a Golden Fleece but a Lamb.

Against all odds, and eccentric to the dualist picture
of intrinsic enmity between spirit and matter, the early
Christians gathered to offer the sacrifice of the Lamb.
It was a magnificent defiance of the Aristotelian longing
for an ephemeral body united to a universal gallantry
called a spirit. The ancient Attic longing was a cerebral
spiritualism, a lofty kind of eclectic religiosity, and the
Christians' opposition to it seemed positively atheistic in
the eyes of the moralists. You could say that the phenomenon is best understood by the heroic tenacity with
which the Christians defined themselves by a Eucharist
instead of a seance. The celebration of the Eucharistic
sacrifice of the Lamb which invokes the presence of the
risen Christ gave the celebrants an immeasurable advantage over their peers gazing on porcelain gods in
pantheons, much as a Christian today at Mass is blessedly
rescued from the indignity of making idols out of
thoughts, like a fervid Ethical Culturist or Leninist. The
Christian "puts on" immortality by receiving into his
own body as a temple the One who is Immortality. Here,
by the way, is asserted almost nonchalantly the revolu-
tionary principle of spiritual science, namely, that immortality is "obtained." We cannot very well put on our
own body because it is intrinsic to our own *ontos,* or
being. We are not born immortal, and we are not a

variety of garden perennial, much greeting card poetry notwithstanding; nor do we "live on" in some opaque echo of our temporal declamations, many eulogies notwithstanding. Immortality is an endowment and mortals are free to decline the inheritance.

Natural observation and deduction alone cannot describe this "putting on" of immortal life. Resurrection is the province of revealed theology. But this does not completely divide the interests of the two kinds of knowledge. Anthropology and psychology limit their own significance when they exclude the implications of life after death. Without a plausible metaphorical reference, only behaviorism and pathology would be at their disposal to explain the persistent whisper which says there is a point *to* the point of death, an ultimate sense beguiling the soul to plant gardens in a world of woods, and to plan cities while camped in caravans.

Since by the very fact of our creation we have an external reference, and since that reference is also transcendent, it alone can complete the picture of immortality which intuition has given us. That transcendent verification of the collective human unconscious is a gift graciously given, and in fact we do call it grace, the materialization of gratuitousness itself. Now St. Paul, we remember, distinguished between "present nature," which is the body, and "mortal nature," which is humanness. The former cannot become free of dying until the latter becomes free of death itself, for the former is a consequence, and not the cause, of the latter. I die because Adam, who is everyone including me, first died and passes on his death each time we try to pass on our life. Original sin basically is inherited mortality.

The grace by which I may recover from death operates only in consequence of the source of grace who is

God killing death itself: "As in Adam all die, so in Christ shall all be made alive." (*I Cor. 15:22*) For man to be "made alive," it is evident that he must first "die" to something. No life can be unless something else yields to it. In the moral order, pride has an obligation to die so that humility can be born. In the physical order, childlessness must die for a child to be born, or as the Celt would put it, "barrenness yields to bairn." A death like this constitutes no material offense since instead of sealing what dies, it replaces it. More graphically, it consumes it. This is why heaven is a feast, and all life truly lived is a Eucharist in which "Christ has died, Christ is risen, Christ will come again." The plaintiff tone, "Come, sweet death," in context is but a pre-prandial version of the festal "Maranatha," "Come," called to Christ the Victor: "Death is swallowed up in victory." (*I Cor. 15:54*)

The Gospel according to St. John, the paramount evangelist of Passover history, devotes five of his twenty-one chapters to this eucharistic phenomenon. Not once is it presented as myth. To be deathless in a eucharistic way very much requires an actual death, quite as a runner's breathlessness makes him gasp for breath. This is just a sign of the more remarkable way by which dying a Christian death cancels lifelessness in the higher reaches of God's hallowed economy.

Grammar's law that two negatives make a positive is quite literally the case in the divine operation of the living Word. In the transcendent grammar, the rubrics do not direct "to be said or sung" inasmuch as all is sung and harmony is not a negligible option; and by this grammar, the crucifixion of the God-Man is the definitively positive act. The "consummatum est" is the central declaration that history has meaning. Only Christ's mother and St. John, she of innocent obedience and he of innocent youth, remained to attend this singular operation by which death was killed. Then in the literary balance of divine events, the first evidence of this life made alive was vouchsafed to Mary Magdalene who had attained a veritable distinction by her lack of innocence. She rounds out the grammar by representing the moral consequences of death's death, for that singular death enables mortals to be forgiven those acts of contradiction which cancel the moral life, to be absolved from those disobediences to the harmony between human desire and divine Will.

The moral order is more than a legal network externally imposed on the conscience. Such would be mere willfulness on the part of the divine Will. The moral order is intrinsic to the human condition; we are only free to violate it in the sense that we are free to reject freedom. Immorality is a slavery to forces inhuman, namely disobedience and concupiscence. The grim lie is the one which says sin is "only human." That is just about the clearest definition of what it is not. The only human acts are positive moral acts which develop the human personality according to its characteristic reality willed by God. The physical resurrection of the body, therefore, is impossible without the moral resurrection of the soul which takes place as its sins are absolved.

There is a difference between the humanitarian and the saint; goodness is something short of holiness. Goodness is obedience to moral law. Holiness is union with the divine source of the law. The difference is based on that identity with Christ's resurrection which comes through forgiveness by Christ. In this order, those whose defective human acts are forgiven are better off than any creature incapable of human acts in the first place. It is finer to be Lazarus in the mould of his shroud than to flourish free of toil as the lilies of the field.

Apollo could not die in myth, and Gabriel cannot sin in fact, but a human can. And so man is neither so melancholy as a god homesick for his Olympian retreat nor so ethereal as an angel who never was away from home. But each child of Adam from his dirt can anticipate the pleasure of a good hot bath at the end of the day, and in his isolation can know the consolation of a friend's welcome. To be a child of Adam is to stand on a precipice, but any precipice has a double view, and the recognition of our relation to Adam is a confirmation that we are also children of God. It is only because we can fall that we can rise; it is only because we are subject to the law of gravity that we can break the law of the grave; it is only because we can be stripped of the good that we can be "clothed with glory and honor;" and it is only because we have been so homeless in what we choose to call history that we are promised beyond history a house with many rooms. It is not our mortality that deters us, but the guilt of mortality. "All the perfume of Arabia" cannot cover it, but only pride is blind to the Arabia beyond Arabia.

The collective unconscious of the human race achieves a sensible account of history when it becomes conscious of God's account of the human race. Then the unconscious motives of human experience enter a spiritual maturity which will not be dismissed as a compulsive neurosis, as the Freudians tried to do to all religions. In that conversion to maturity, the "trumpet will sound" and it will be understood for what it is, not a silver alarm to disarray, but a fading breath, a leaf falling sooner than expected before winter, a thud of earth upon a box opening a consciousness for which deep human wisdom long yearns:

Wake, awake, for night is flying:
The watchmen on the heights are crying,
Awake, Jerusalem, arise!
Midnight's solemn hour is tolling,
His chariot wheels are nearer rolling . . .

Mortal somnolence does not like being awakened for nothing; but even less does it like awakening to nothing. Some sleeplessness is caused by the anxious fear that there may be no state beyond sleep. If the truth were told more often instead of being couched in allegory, everyone would understand why the most alarming thought is the prospect of nothing surprising us. This is why in the old fairy tales the witch causes slumber and the prince startles from sleep. The psychologist knows that the myriad anxieties recumbant in children's fables are expressed the way they are because children can empathize with characters before mastering the expression of their own character. Adults have their own fables which do not look fabulous at all. Romances on the soap operas are hardly romantic, but that does not mean they are realistic as their producers claim. They are one with the classic fabulists in the evasive fear that there might be no kiss to awaken the kingdom, no sun in the palace where dawn was supposed to appear.

At "midnight's solemn hour" the problem is one o'clock; then one o'clock yields to two. When responsible people worry about economic injustice, crime in the streets, the appalling nuclear peril, they conceal their fear of the hour past midnight less artfully than the hymnwriters and storytellers. For there is a deep story behind the daily news, a long sickness behind the social ills, and it has to do with what moved Cain to strike Abel. Social disharmony can be called sin only analogously. To speak of social sins as if there really were such things is to skirt around the fact that only humans sin, structures do not. In the most enlightened moral sense, social structures may be invaded by sin, but in themselves they are occasions for telling that deeper story which is the burden of every child born to Adam.

Social reconstructionists could discuss nothing more vital to their aims than the noise of a falling leaf; for if utopia were established and every sword beaten into a plowshare, autumn would sound louder than ever. Were there no missiles there would still be Mortmain. If all bombs were dismantled, the ticking sound would still continue; bombs are easier to defuse than calendars and it is simpler to disarm a battalion than to take the arms from a clock. Utopia would still seem a dark kingdom with the night a shroud and every chime a toll. Dostoevsky's warning about our lack of intellectual preparedness for great events was concerned about this. So was Solzhenitsyn when he warned the West against preferring anaesthetic to responsibility; and the West received his words with a silence which corroborated him.

The difference between boredom and eternity is the difference between anxiety and awareness, and the secular humanist is in a tenuous state between the two. He recognizes that the greatest people alive have an intuition of something beyond death, while at the same time he is bound by a moral tether to those commitments which several generations of liberal progressivism have placed upon him, and which deny that very intuition. The "end of the human race as we know it," which causes the secularist such fits, is not the end of the human race as we should know it. The human race has two ends, not as a string has ends, but as does anything with a destiny as well as a terminus. Science is capable of grasping this; scientism is not. Science moves toward conclusions, while scientism assumes, with not a shred of scientific proof, that a conclusion is a finale. Another term for the error as it assumes philosophical proportions is existentialism. Practical people usually are too broadminded to indulge it. Ask the Commissioner of Transportation the end of the subway and he will say it is to help commuters commute; ask commuters and they will say it is the Bronx. It would not occur to either to deny the other, as would some members of the intellegentsia who have been educated beyond their intelligence. A nutritionist knows that the end of a meal is nutrition, but he may simultaneously be a gourmand who calls it dessert. The complementarity of the two simply ensures that the end will be recognized when it is reached. Otherwise, the result is an hypocrisy against the self; that selfhood has to be part of two ends whether or not they are acknowledged. "Hypocrites! You know how to interpret the appearance of earth and sky; but why do you not know how to interpret the present time?" (*Luke 12:56*)

Christ has known the purpose of time, and it was Christ who loved his own who were in the world "to the end." (*John 13:1*) This deep, transcendent love was a conflation of the completion and the purpose of life; it brought together the double end of chronological time, *kronos*, and moral time, *kairos*, in the only way that these can be united if the human race is to achieve authentic fulfillment. The chronological end of life entered into its "fullness" of purpose when the Lord of Time welcomed his end on the cross with words which mean both "It is finished" and "It is accomplished".

The hypocrisy is not so discernable when it takes the form of schizophrenia. It is no less of a betrayal. It is endemic to the movements of one kind or another which claim to liberate in the social order without offering moral freedom. One need only compare the Byzantine music of the Easter Liturgy in St. Petersburg with the melancholy recording of a violin in the cavernous war memorial mausoleum in Leningrad. We need not go that far abroad to encounter it. The cloying enthusiasm of a grain-fed, pink-cheeked American choir singing "This Land is Your Land, This Land is My Land" can be far more effusive, and for that reason decidedly more cholic, than the Gregorian mode of "Laetare, Jerusalem." But an indigenized Christ will always seem cheerier than the real one who had no place to lay his head. Many contemporary films, plays and novels portray the silent rage of people oblivious to their lack of place for the prophetic Christ of the Gospel; and the substitute *deus ex machina* is probably more often than not a psychiatrist who at his best can only measure the decibles of that discontent. A parable for it is in the teenaged rock fan who thought her record amplifier was broken; she was relieved to be told that she was only losing her hearing.

To deny sin as a factor in the mortal condition is no more realistic than to solve death by denying that it happens, as did Mary Baker Eddy. She believed her theory as genuinely as her death refuted it. Sincerity of conviction in the urbane conscience today is no more successful, even as it deals with forms of dying in fragments: gossip, selfish competition, divorce, artificial contraception, drug abuse. Pope Paul made no miscalculation in his encyclical *Humanae Vitae*, except to understate the consequences of the contraceptive mentality. With unpredictable swiftness it has ushered in the contradiction of creative power in many forms, including increased abortions, infanticide, child abuse, adultery, euthanasia and, it should be added, a decrease in religious vocations, because contraceptive parents are not in a position of generosity to raise up consecrated children. At the current low reproductive rate, Western Culture is in danger of self-destruction; by the year 2100 there will be 20 million Germans compared with 62 million today; the rate is little better in the United States where one third of the 54 million women of childbearing age are incapable of having children, half of these because of sterilization. This, along with illegitimate births which increase as the use of contraceptives increases, represent the facts, even when they are ignored by groups illogical enough to propose contraception as a preventive for the very problems it exacerbates.

Apart from Christ's power to kill death, each vestige of human existence becomes a species of victimization: "These are blemishes on your love feasts, as they boldly carouse together, looking after themselves; waterless clouds, carried along by winds; fruitless trees in late autumn, twice dead, uprooted; wild waves of the sea, casting upon the foam of their own shame; wandering stars for whom the nether gloom of darkness has been reserved for ever." (*Jude 12-13*)

In the exasperation of its victim status, the human race has committed three acts against God since the Fall which have been of ascending pridefulness. First, the pre-Christians tried to redesign God. Second, the anti-Christians tried to kill God. Third, the post-Christians tried to declare God dead of natural causes. One weekly magazine, which a few years ago suggested that the Age of Belief had been replaced by the Age of Man, recently named the computer Man of the Year. Neither God nor Man has faded away but, in frustration with mortality, life has gone out of human definitions. Of course "post-Christianity" describes only a cultural bias, not an historical fact; Christ is the perduring motive of history and there can be nothing "after him." He has followers but no sequel.

For the sake of discussion, suppose that God had indeed died. This is an oxymoron, but allow it for the purpose of the moment. It is known that God the Son did once die and the result was life after death. But even when God the Son died, divinity did not die. As God is Life, the death of Life would not give life to death; it would eradicate existence. To grapple with inadequate words, existence subsists in "istence." Theologians call this self-sufficiency "aseity," but any symbol will do. Without it there would be no possibility of supposing anything at all. An eclipse does not eliminate the sun, but the elimination of the sun would more than eclipse us. Yet let us persist in contradiction and pretend that one might see the annihilation of God. The Prince of Lies alone has the invention of contradiction to try it; only He-Who-Is-Against is not reversed when he looks at a mirror. He reads the Prologue of Life the only way he ever found legible:

> In the End was Silence,
> And the Silence was against God and the Silence was
>   not God.
> Through it nothing came to be.
> All things died because of it.
> And that death was the dark of men.
> A night that enters into the light,
> A darkness that light could not overcome.

It is a talisman of the most hideous kind, or at least it would be if we lacked straight eyes and straighter reason. At one moment in the human story a figure made history, and he did not do it as the notables surrounding him did. While the local bureaucrats were making history, he was constructing it. The Church has the right Prologue today, and not Satan's, because of this: into the midst of the many who believed that they knew as well as anyone else the way to true life, one entered who could legitimately say that he was the Way, the Truth, and the Life.

His instrument is the voice which contradicts the conceit of silence. In Galilee it did not sound inflated, like various news commentators and philosophers with tenure. Some of those who heard it were scandalized by the nonchalance with which the voice cast asides about the tragedy of death: "Follow me, and let the dead bury their dead." (*Matt. 8:22*) But it was not callous as all that. These deaths would pass; what moved the voice, indeed moved it so that the timbre ached, was the sorrow of those who were still alive. The incarnation would have been nothing more than a broker–client operation had Christ not felt their loss. His voice preached every form of sermon except a eulogy; but he did not reveal more of the covenant between heaven and earth than when he wept at the death of a friend and groaned at his tomb. He called his cousin a saint but he thought it more to the point to call the one who killed his cousin a fox. At Nain, the sight of a young man's corpse did not stir him to action; to his way of thinking it would have been like stopping the youth from entering college. He was moved by the lament of the youth's mother.

This inconsolable longing, when there was no longing in heaven, arrested his glance. Rachel wept for her children for they were no more, but he wept because it was not clear to Rachel how they still were and would be. In his passion, nails were as nothing compared to the wail-

ing of the daughters of Jerusalem; their weeping for
him was undue. In all its horror, the tears of his own
mother at his crucified feet were a comfort, for she was
not mourning; quite the contrary, she was weeping for
Jerusalem, which Jerusalem itself would not do.

During the earthly ministry, Jesus resuscitated the
dead. Occasional resuscitations are not eternal resur-
rections. Lazarus, and the widow's son, and the "sleep-
ing" daughter of Jairus, would die again. The motive
was to conquer loneliness, not death. He erased the
punctuation point of death, but death, an assiduous
grammarian if not a lyricist, replaced it soon enough.
Our Lord's confidence in these moments might have
been a stolidity of tragic potential, indifferent as Zeus
and dispassionate as a dutiful tycoon, had there been no
great secret behind it. But as it was, the point of death
did not intimidate him because he could see the point
to death. It was not a matter of seeing around an obstacle; it was more like seeing through an enemy. The
process of it was even beyond his own determination:
"So they took away the stone. And Jesus lifted his eyes
and said, 'Father, I thank thee that thou hast heard me.
I know that thou hearest me always, but I have said this
on account of the people standing by, that they may
believe that thou didst send me.' " (*John 11:41-42*)

His obedience to the proceedings moved his death
into a unique category, neither suicide nor tragedy, neither murder nor heroic martyrdom. Nor was his certitude based on what he remembered of history or
foresaw of the future, for the essential Christ is neither
Sage nor Seer, neither Remembrancer nor Foreteller,
but the Fact of Experience itself: "I am." The truth about
his death is that it was true; the way he died was the only
way he could, and the life that died was the only life

there is. Caiaphas the high priest said more than he realized when he remarked how it was better that Jesus should die than that everyone else should die. In Christ's crucifixion the past, present, and future meet in mutual significance, for Christ at the point of death is the point to death: "I am the beginning and the end." (*Rev. 1:8; 21:6; 22:13*)

Recognizing this no more resolves the mystery than does ignoring it, but a supernatural mystery is not a puzzle to be pieced together, anyway. Even if you could put Humpty Dumpty back together again, all you would get is Humpty Dumpty. Nor is a supernatural mystery anything like a detective story that explains who stabbed the millionaire in the rose bushes. It is its own kind of mystery, a fact from a larger world which looks perfectly ordinary, when in actuality it is imperfectly ordinary, until human eyes adjust to see it the way God does. Blake said: "They ever must believe a lie/Who see with, not though, the eye."

Death and life seem puzzling, even though St. Paul said he was showing in them a mystery, because only divine intentiveness can fully divine their intentions. Christ Risen was not recognized by his closest friends at first. Rather than yield to frustration or agnosticism, the soul takes consolation in St. Augustine's reminder: *Non enim fecit et abiit.* That is to say, God did not go to the length of creating our world only to abandon it.

A mystery needs patience to be valued, and patience is equivalent to vision in the divine order. Divine patience sees every sparrow that falls to the ground. This is not poetic expression; it is God's own description of facts. Now patience is a sister virtue to humility, and the patience of God is equally a sign of his humble accessibility to what he has made. Mystery is obscured only when humility is obscured. The saints have understood this as the truth of all truths in the interior life: spiritual shortsightedness comes from spiritual smallmindedness, and spiritual blindness is the disease of pride. "For judgement I came into this world, that those who do not see may see, and that those who see may become blind." (*John 9:39*) It is not that the spiritually blind cannot see; this blindness is an inability to see its blindness, a case of the idol's affliction: "Having eyes they see not." (*Psalm 135:16*) Often those with the sharpest eyesight are blind that way. In that case the naked eye is not acute but bare; instead of the eye of an artist, it becomes the eye of the aesthete who calls "dirt" on the West Side, "patina" on the East Side, and climbs over wrecks to spot a ruin. God, as author of beauty, does not condescend to treat us as a work of art. Instead, when he wants us to brighten our vision of the eternally beautiful, he enjoins us, "Harden not your hearts . . ." (*Psalm 95:8*); that hardening is the fiercest *rigor mortis*, barring the soul from all beauty, truth, and goodness, and blinding it to the depths beyond death. God knows what is in the heart of man by knowing what is at the heart of man, and this knowledge alone is the mystery we are allowed to perceive.

At the heart, then, is a double facet to death, since death is both physical and moral. Deep death came not by man holding a sword or a gun; it came by man himself. Consequently, the death of death is effected not by a man holding a new weapon but by a new man: "For as by a man came death, so also by a man has come the resurrection of the dead." (*I Cor. 15:21*) The man who introduced death to life was Adam, a name which means

"The Man." Now The Man was created by The God; and so, in the mystery, humanity can only be saved from death by the source of the breath first breathed into The Man. The refrain then begins to make more sense: "As in Adam all die, even so in Christ shall all be made alive." (*I Cor. 15:22*)

It is tempting, and almost probable, to conjecture that this moral aspect of death is only theoretical. As an abstraction, it seems less immediate a concern than physical death. The death of Adam does not seem in any ordinary experience as devastating as my being hit by a car. On such occasions even theologians tend to forget about Adam. But, if we are to believe it, there is a long distance pain worse than the short distance pain, and we cannot believe it until we have gone the distance. There is some intimation of it in the hierarchy of lesser pain; experience does seem to teach that a personal hurt is not quite so painful a thing as watching someone whom we love in pain. Even more devastating is the remorse at having personally hurt someone beloved.

As the New Man, Christ's crucifixion was painful beyond that of any other, though it took no more nails than for the other thousands crucified in that age. Many have had to submit to physical punishment which was even more sadistic. It is one thing, though, to measure the punishment and another to measure the pain. The suffering of Christ was unfathomable because his wound felt the wound of the world, sweating Adam's sweat as the sons of Adam offered him rotten wine from below. The cup he had foreseen and tried to pray away was a mixture of bitterness, made of Dachau's barbed wire and filled with the blood of Flanders crying from the flayed ground. The *Alpha* in him knew the *Omega*. His carpenter's hand was forced to feel Cain's heavy club.

His fingers that once beckoned children are wrapped daily around the abortionist's glacial scalpel. It is all one moment with him; the *Omega* ends the allegory. The blood he sweat was not a figure of speech; and given the moral death being undone, he could have cried blood, too.

Any way you look at it, an exit from the puzzle is an entrance into the mystery. A man extricates himself from a maze only to be implicated in a world. Such is what the Church calls baptism into Christ's death. Famous figures in history are said to survive in their followers, but the followers of Christ survive in him. He has a following precisely because nothing follows him. He is the Church without end, into which baptism is the entrance, not only by initiation, but by that absolution from sin which is nothing less than regeneration, or rebirth. His followers are "united with Christ in the Church and marked by the Holy Spirit who is the assurance of our inheritance." (*Lumen Gentium*, N. 48; see also *Eph. 1:14*)

If this does not move the conscience beyond what St. Augustine called the "obscurity of a similitude," that is, inadequacy of literal description, there is no reason to take a wait-and-see position. No one can genuinely hope against hope that this "dying with Christ" is less final than the approach of the moth to the flame. It is not possible to "wait and see" what the mystery portends, for neither man nor death is static. Rather, human courage has to step through it, like Alice Through the Looking Glass or, in fact, like the Hebrews Through the Wilderness. Only then can the personality expect to know that implicit trust is more than fruitless self-projection, or the passionless trance of Satan who stares at a mirror he cannot enter.

THE POINT OF DEATH 57

"One step enough" was the young Newman's entry into the mystery, but the important thing is that it was a step. The contemplation of finality, if it is to be an interior reality of the soul, has also to be participation: "I die daily." (*I Cor. 15:31*) The people of the Hebrews had in fact left the Egyptian concept of immortality behind them, and brought no belief in life after death with them when they entered the wilderness. But by entering that desert they also embarked upon an encounter which eventually brought them to an experience of an eternity far more vital than the stagnant deathlessness of their former taskmasters. Trust flung them into cataracts of tribulations, but the one of which they were free was the melancholia of the skeptic. Because he has never entered a scene, the skeptic cannot be sure whether it is true or a mirage.

Limpid representations of Christ are the artifice of remote observers who do not take seriously the Christian command to take up a cross daily. The deep mystery of death and its consequences is the mystery of exile; and unless the soul considers the devastating potency of alienation it will not be able to recognize the true home on the other side of the desert. That wistfulness complected Mr. Fearing in *Pilgrim's Progress* until he was "dumpish" even in the House Beautiful. It is possible to become so domestic that we lose our sense of home in the preoccupation with having a house.

In the last century, the sometimes stifling domesticity of the Regency household produced etchings of young women drooping fern-like over funerary urns. They were supposed to be Christian, but that does not change the vast difference between them and the bright red and ochre resurrection scenes in the early Christian catacombs. The distinction is one between the "rendezvous

with death" attitude and the covenant attitude. As God
promised Abraham, only the consciousness of a covenant can justify confidence in the keeping of a promise
and the assurance of a good end. One approaches a
rendezvous but one enters a covenant, and the distinction is as great a divide as that between a suitor and a
spouse.

When men and women say they are "absolutely mortified," whatever else they mean, they are not mortified
the way saints are. For holy mortification is hardly a
sudden shock. It is very much a regular exercise to prevent shock. There are two ways to break an egg: smash
the outside in anger, which is not a form of mortification
but destruction; or crack it to let the inside become the
outside, which is precisely what the saints have regularly
done. In so doing, they have shown in a mystical way
how the outpouring of a soul fills the soul. To the objection that mortification is sadistic, every saintly life can
answer for itself that sadism is just what mortification
avoids. Sadism plays with pain and death while mortification attacks them. Among the aspirations of the
saints, there is this uttered by Catherine of Siena in her
last agony: "I will suffering to be my food, tears my
drink, sweat my ointment. Let suffering fatten me, suffering heal me, suffering give me light, suffering give
me wisdom, suffering clothe my nakedness, suffering
divest me of all self-love, spiritual and temporal."

Mortification is a prayer of the senses, as Josemaria
Escrivá taught, a communication between the fact of
mortality and the source of potential immortality. Joy
is an indispensable evidence of sanctity, or spiritual
wholeness, because mortification is the ruination of morbidity. Morbidity is the product of misread creation.
Secularism offers countless examples of morbid person-

alities, the saints not one. Morbidity is preoccupation with death, but the saints avoid that by their occupation with death, a lifelong work devoted to defeating it. In this interior life there is a brilliant practicality which preserves the covenant with life, even when the unbeliever offers many plausible myths about a rendezvous with death. These are invalid myths because they suggest that death has some vitality over life. Death is death definitively because it has no vitality, not anymore than a shadow has blood. We all must meet death, but we cannot hold a meeting with it. The only one who ever did was Christ, and so his death is called the Passion.

Until the conscience recognizes that the soul is as real as the body, it will value mortification only when it is practiced in connection with the body. Any serious person practices self-denial. The question is whether it will be limited to dieting for the purpose of slimness and exercise for increasing endurance, or whether extended to include fasting for the sake of mastery over gluttony, together with spiritual exercises such as vigils and good works. Onerous tasks should be accepted in order to increase the spiritual stamina for enduring the longer race which, St. Paul told the Corinthians, aims at the goal of all living. The Church has long used the term Ascetical Theology for the study of this phenomenon, drawing on the Greek word which means exercise, so that the discus thrower and the Christian at prayer both are athletes. If there is any contrast, it is that the spiritual athlete takes the exercise more seriously; and this is only to be expected since his opponent in the amphitheater is more likely than not a lion. "Be sober, be watchful. Your adversary the devil prowls around like a roaring lion, seeking someone to devour. Resist him, firm in your faith, knowing that the same experience of suffering is required of your brotherhood throughout the world. And after you have suffered a little while, the God of all grace, who has called you to his eternal glory in Christ, will himself restore, establish, and strengthen you." (*I Peter 5:8-10*)

The strengthening is evident enough from a moral view. The ability to love another appears when mortification kills lust; gratification from long lasting truths is felt when greed is mortified; character becomes more vibrant when selfishness dies; hope prevails when the will turns into willpower which crushes the illusion of futility. Without a denial of self-will the soul becomes possessed by those very gifts it was meant to possess. Vanity is a humiliation for this very reason; it reduces the individual to the obsessive conviction that human integrity depends on everything except humanity. Vain people think so little of themselves that they shrink from the light when wrinkles appear, and jump from office windows then they lose an account. This led to our Lord's uncommon opinion that deprivation might be enriching: "So therefore, whoever of you does not renounce all that he has cannot be my disciple." (*Luke 14:33*) He means an economics in which the amount of money is quite immaterial and the amount of freedom is absolutely material.

The cost of discipleship is a matter of possessing far more than possessions. In the long train of disciples, some were rich in pocket and poor in spirit, like Lazarus and the centurion and Joseph of Arimaethea. Poverty of spirit is a state of detachment. The rich young man was sent away for his very lack of that endowment. His problem, which he let become a sin, was that instead of being a young man who was rich, he thought of himself as riches in the form of a young man.

Jesus counted poor and rich among his friends; he loved humanity so perfectly that he had to leave out the voluntarily dehumanized who were not so much attached to the nonhuman as they were captivated by it. By such a process, symbolized in Genesis by the attraction of the fruit of the forbidden tree, death got a control over the human condition which it was never meant to have. Whether some kind of temporal death was part of the original divine plan for creation is a moot point. It may have been, though we cannot be sure, that even before the Fall the first man and woman were stuck with death as we are. The tragedy came in the Fall when they became stuck *to* death. That is the captivity against which all temporal mortifications protest, and from which the Detachment of Christ came to set us free. He never insisted that man die poor; but he strictly forbade man to die poorly.

The negative force of mortification, which obtains through detachment, renunciation and eradication, has therefore, as cooperative in God's will for man, a positive force which renders it operative. Otherwise it would, so to speak, short-circuit spiritual growth, as is the case with the masochist. Because mortification in the sacramental economy is different from that masochism, an enormous divide exists between the Catholic and the Puritan. It is a distinction confused sometimes even by the "muscular Christianity" first proposed by the heartier evangelicals in the last century. Even an Irish monk standing in a cold stream to win Heaven is not so uncongenial to civilized sense as is a football player taking a cold shower for Christ so that he might win a game. The same Paul who was not loathe to athletic equations well knew the perils of that particular kind of piety which confuses doing good and doing well: "For if you live according to the flesh, you shall die; but if by the Spirit you mortify the deeds of the flesh, you shall live." (*Rom. 8:13*)

Religiosity as an attempt at spiritual consolations without the threatening implications of mortal sacrifice creates a self-defeating restlessness. This tends to be the type of religious philosophy most marketable in the modern consumerist society. Characteristically bourgeois, it breathes best in a specialized Protestant climate, although the sixteenth century examples of Gallicans like Boileau and Nicole set a precedent for modern progressivist Catholics who take to it; but American materialism is far more contradictory to the sacramental vision than classical Gallicanism ever was. Its ambition for an independent "American Catholicism" is a thoroughly bourgeois flight from the Roman and Apostolic man who takes the Kingdom of Heaven by force.

The self-protecting religionist who hesitates to enter the economy of sacrifice soon will not want to enter the confessional and then he will not want to enter the church. Indeed, he may embark on those most transient emotional gratifications, inventing what are said to be "meaningful worship experiences" with "theme" liturgies, turning the sanctuary into something closely resembling a cocktail lounge, or just "watching church" on television. The actual concept of watching church is symptomatic of a spiritual schizophrenia; in light of the mystery whereby the Church is the body of Christ, this is a morose delectation when it is taken seriously. Allowably, it saves the conscience from dealing with deep questions, but only staring at those questions also deprives that conscience of many deep answers. Doubting Thomas made it to Heaven; there is no evidence that Peeping Tom did.

The interior life of the soul condemns itself to the

realm of illusion when it becomes a spectator sport and dissipates the ability for profound articulation of the human experience. Mortification as a prayer of the senses helps prevent such a subjectivized piety by directing those elements of the personality which are vital to deep thought and which, when neglected, give rise to a malaise of perception. As the disciples of Christ are called to relinquish possessiveness, they free themselves from sensual captivity only by disciplining their own senses through individual acts of mortification. The exterior senses so controlled are the sight, hearing and speech; the interior senses are imagination and memory; the higher faculties are intellect and will. The social dimension of this discipline helps to avoid the egocentrism of the religious pietist who distrusts creation and the secular self-affirmationist who distrusts any Creator. "Now I rejoice in my sufferings for your sake, and in my flesh I complete what is lacking in Christ's afflictions for the sake of his body, that is, the church . . ." (*Col. 1:24*)

Without these exercises of our freedom, the soul is sort of suspended in an indifferent languor, increasingly incapable of ordering the senses. Then the emotions of which we are capable begin to go out of control. These, generally speaking, are those feelings of deep longing: the concupiscible appetites of love, hatred, desire, aversion, joy and sadness; and the irascible, or readily conditioned, appetites of courage, fear, hope, despair and anger. The most vague idealist is likely to understand the need to control these; but the thought of mortifying them, that is to render them accountable to a purpose beyond death, must seem as senseless as death itself. But death only appears senseless when humans refuse to mortify their senses themselves.

That refusal produces the most senseless conclusion

of all, namely, that God is dead. But such senselessness
is tolerable when the senses have been embalmed instead
of mortified. And what can this mean, unless it is that
senses embalmed are senses morally indifferent to the
great ends of life? It would be better to announce an
honest preference for distorted passion than to deny its
power to captivate the soul and then confect a religion
whose god justifies my sins rather than myself. Joseph
Conrad said God is for men and religion for women;
but in fact men and women have a mutual choice, not
between the two, but between the revealed religion
based on a god, and the projected god based on a religion.

Of course it cannot be black and white as all that and
still be supernatural, because nothing known about God
has been black and white. The logical positivist may
think it has, in spite of the fact that it is just as logical
for a negative to come out black and white. Transcen-
dental judgment achieves its lucidity through an attach-
ment to eternal clarity; for clarity, and not simple
contrast, is what revelation gives the intellect.

God intends that human perception be grounded in
reference and not reflex, and that reference must be to
a higher order of being beyond the grave. As that true
picture develops, the colors develop too. And so it is
with the passions. Through mortification, they are capable of becoming greater than mere reflexes. They can
actually be trained to assume a vibrancy such that will
enable the impassioned spirit to tolerate the one color
of the spectrum not tolerable to earthly sense, the glory
which the carnal eye of pride does not consider a color
at all. This should not daunt the beginner, because pride
never thought purity might be colorful either.

The very thought may seem shocking nevertheless,

but that is an encouraging sign. The sophisticate's inability to be shocked is an insufferable ability to be bored. When boredom becomes a way of life, it also becomes hard to draw a line between death and life. Mortification, aided by indispensable grace, allowed the saints to subsume all their passion under the fundamental love-passion which, as Bossuet said, is the stimulant of all the others. St. Thomas called love the form of all virtues; it is not a solitary virtue but needs the virtues as vehicles. And love without the life of the virtues is only a secular sentimentalism. Consequently, and much to the frustration of the epicurean, only the saint can love life with pure *passion*.

In the line of thought so far developed, the alternative to holy mortification is neurotic morbidity in which the object of the soul's desire is no longer life but existence. When people stop worshipping the Holy Spirit, they spontaneously make a cult of their own breath. The moral relativist has suggested that this is the right approach, and if that is so, then self-worship is the only suitable religion. But it is also the loneliest religion. In its solitary reverie an unrest persists; even when the passion for life is replaced by a panic for existence, there remains the unanswered question: who or what is the "ist-ness" from which the lonely votary has exited. And the answer will not remain black and white for long.

Contemplation of death, the *memento mori* of which only humans are capable, precludes any genuine satisfaction with caricatures of holy lives. Saints appear as clichés only to lives lived as clichés, as though life itself were but a quivering neurosis, a breathlessness of which only the worshippers of breath are capable. The saints grown weary lose their breath as readily as anyone else, but there are two kinds of breathlessness, and theirs is one of awe and not vapidity. Saint Francis whispered his welcome to "Sister Death," in awe not of her, but of a youth that can age, of a change that happens at the moment when all happening is supposed to cease, of a stillness as riveting as the former motion, of an absence as palpable as a presence, of a peace the intimation of which indicates harmony and, if harmony, then music.

Gone now are many of those who taught us how to walk and how to eat, and first spoke of right and wrong. Are they now unreal? If they seem to be unreal, surely our walking and eating and moral discernment remain. And if we no longer wear the clothes of our childhood, we still wear about us the sense of those departed figures who once in our lives tied our shoelaces and buttoned our first winter coats. Now that we are tall and warm, does it mean that they must be gone and cold? Did Abraham yield to Isaac and Isaac to Jacob like some rod in a relay race, and can our parents say nothing beyond the point of death unless we say it for them? Are songs a thousand years old still sung, but songwriters a thousand years old now nothing? And is the New Adam dead with the Old, splintered as his cross and crumbling as his bread?

Were we dead, we could not say yea or nay to the reality of experience, and as we are alive we cannot say yea to its denial. We are left to reply a certain nay to absurdity in the persistent grammar of sense; and the sound of it contradicts the first nay to sensibility that shattered Eden's shining peace. And as the grammar goes, there is born of the double nay an affirmation which cannot be located, but which stands at the point of every point the conscience ever tries to make: "Yea, though I walk through the valley of the shadow of death I will fear no evil: for thou art with me, thy rod and thy staff they comfort me." (*Psalm 23:4*)

Praise to the Holiest in the height, And in the depth
   be praise;
In all his words most wonderful, Most sure in all his
   ways!

O loving wisdom of our God! When all was sin and
   shame,
A second Adam to the fight, And to the rescue came.

O wisest love! that flesh and blood, Which did in
   Adam fail,
Should strive afresh against the foe, Should strive and
   should prevail;

And that a higher gift than grace Should flesh and
   blood refine:
God's presence and his very self, And essence all divine.
O generous love! that he who smote In Man for man
   the foe,
The double agony in Man For man should undergo;

And in the garden secretly, And on the cross on high,
Should teach his brethren, and inspire To suffer and
   to die.

Praise to the Holiest in the height, And in the depth
   be praise:
In all his words most wonderful, Most sure in all his
   ways!

John Henry Newman, 1865

TWO

JUDGEMENT

The Father judges no one, but has given all judgement
to the Son, that all may honor the Son, even as they
honor the Father. He who does not honor the Son
does not honor the Father who sent him. Verily, verily, I say to you, he who hears my word and believes
him who sent me has eternal life; he does not come
into judgment, but has passed from death to life.
Verily, verily, I say to you, the hour is coming, and
now is, when the dead will hear the voice of the Son
of God, and those who hear will live. For as the Father
has life in himself, so he has granted the Son also to
have life in himself, and has given him authority to
execute judgement, because he is the Son of man. Do
not marvel at this; for the hour is coming when all
who are in the tombs will hear his voice and come
forth, those who have done good, to the resurrection
of life, and those who have done evil, to the resurrection of judgement. (*John 5:22-29*)

The corollary of the idea that there is no right or

wrong says that what matters is how you may get away with it. The "it" inevitably is the wrong, for only a rare soul plots how to get away with the good. Since even among atheists a residue of Christian reference remains, like confetti after a wedding, there is a pious version of this which says you may do whatever you want so long as you do not hurt anyone. But it is the same anti-social solipsism, and its most dangerous contribution to ethics is the way its combination of egoism and utilitarianism has obliterated any distinction between the verbs *can* and *may*.

This is exactly the confusion indicated in the excuse, "But it's only natural. . . ." The distinction between what we *could* do and what we *might* do is the lingering whisper to every age, dark or golden, which says no act is "only natural." There is a material part of each act which is an operation of nature, but the act also has a form, perceived and directed by a will, endowed from outside nature.

Any theory which holds that we *may* do anything we *can* do is about as capable of holding water as the sieves of the constrained Danaids in classical myth; and anyone who tries to make the theory work will find himself in the labyrinthine underworld of illogic. Liberation from sin can be a euphemism for enslavement to vice. The most liberated societies have the highest suicide rates and most morbid obsessions. Such liberation is an obsessiveness totally different from the compulsion which finished Romeo and Juliet; it rejects the romance of cutting ourselves into "little stars" to make the face of heaven fine. Instead, it pursues either fragmented sensory stimulation or total isolationism as an end in itself.

In a juvenile way, this idea is illustrated in the transformation of the folkloric fairy tale into the pedestrianism of Saturday morning cartoons and the condescending vulgarity of children's educational television. From the perspective of history, the balance between ephemeral stimulus and negative withdrawal has been the responsibility of the Church, as it preserved the divine romance from the errors of collectivism and individualism. The contemporary media now take that function of guidance upon themselves and, for the most part, do it badly. An electronically educated society is now evolving into an amalgam of conformity and egoism, producing an unattractive state of affairs in which everyone does "his own thing" exactly as everyone else.

Human acts need a transcendent truth to verify the integrity of the conscience and will which are the constituents of any authentically human activity. Natural law is helpful but not sufficient for judging human acts. All one may reasonably expect of natural law is that it will guide natural acts. Then again, people cannot justify what they do by the natural law alone, since that would not qualify their acts as human. Unnatural acts will of course be inhuman, but the converse does not inevitably obtain, as if naturalness guaranteed humanness. It is "only natural" for a dog to walk naked along Fifth Avenue, and any objection to it would be a case for the pathologist and not the moralist; but it would not be "only natural" for a woman to be naked as she walked the dog, for the simple fact that she has more than nature in her. In that instance it would be of both pathological and moral concern. This is not to diminish the integrity of creation; nor is it to "improve" it. It is rather to transfigure it. Eve in Eden learned that there is more to nature than nature. There is the grace of God and if a human denies this he is not being unnatural, but he is certainly being silly.

Human acts cannot be judged as isolated events, like the Nominalist philosophers tried to do. Even the standard of universal norms is to be respected, but not taken as the ultimate proof of right and wrong. An observer, for instance, may judge that a welfare state is morally inadequate; he may go so far as to suggest that a welfare state is an obstacle to human wellness. This would remain an opinion, and a disputed one at that. Were all the Swedes to kill themselves, other Socialists would blame the mess on a regretable persistence of bourgeois tendencies. A deaf man has his own opinion about the peacock which he calls the loveliest of birds and he cannot understand why the blind man reviles it as the screechiest of birds.

All judgements remain truncated opinions, except for the only kind of judgement which is truly human because it is more than "only natural," and that is divine judgement. Christ was the only perfect judge because, in a manner of speaking, he was able to "see" what human ears can only hear and "hear" what human eyes can only see. Only he who is at the heart of the universe might know what is at the heart of man. To the morally blind personality, the heart cannot exist because it cannot be felt; and to the morally deaf, it cannot exist because it cannot be heard. But the Sacred Heart, which lies deeper than time and space, can touch the human heart by speaking to it, and can hear its cry by letting it touch him. The word for this operation is Incarnation. Alone among all humans could the incarnate God, who heard what his disciples said out of earshot and saw Nathanael under the fig tree out of sight, state without arrogance: "You have heard it said . . . but I say unto you . . ." (*Matt. 5:21-22; 33-34*) So it is that moral judgement, even in the natural order, requires a reference from behind that order. Pascal reminded his naturalist friends that the Scriptures prove nothing about God simply from natural evidence. And it is apparent that we have said some foolish things about ourselves by using nothing other than natural evidence.

A look at the perspective of Scripture presents one puzzle at the start. Our Lord says, "I judge no man," (*John 8:15*) and the next chapter has him saying, "For judgement I came into this world." (*John 9:39*) Even rhetorically, it would be tendentious to ask whether this is the sign of a split personality. No one, not even his contemporary enemies and subsequent critics, all of whom had many charges against him, ever charged him with schizophrenia. The significance of human acts well depends on what he meant when he said that he does and does not judge.

He preached six parables on judgement, and each is so carefully crafted that, in sum, they show all he ever needed those he loves to know about the matter. All else that can ever be said will, rabbinically speaking, be interesting, but still commentary.

The Parable of the Talents (*Matt. 25:14ff*) teaches that men and women will be judged according to what they do with their individuality, for individuals are individual by merit of the gift peculiar to each; to acknowledge this is to attain that positive kind of individualism which delights in the gift. And better, too, will we avoid the defensive individualism which resents the gift in others. The philosopher may call the former a Cartesian realism, associating the *ego* and the *cogito*, the "I" and the "I know," the latter being a divorce of the two. In more cosmic language, St. Paul uses the term "glory" for this cognition; God endows us with individuality and saves us from individualism by bestowing a splendor in each

of us which, like that of the planets in space, forms a
universal reality while differing between each other as
examples. Since there is "one glory of the sun, and another glory of the moon, and another glory of the stars,"
so the gift of maternity differs from the gift of paternity,
wealth from eloquence, power from patience. The divine Giver requires in return only a cooperation with
the order of giving; and this cooperation in fullest degree, animated by the life of the virtues, focused on the
giver and not on the gift, is love. God who is love judges
his creatures whom he loves only by the reciprocity of
their gifts: "Every one to whom much is given, of him
will much be required . . ." (*Luke 12:48*)

"Dollars" and "pounds" do not show the pun in the
old term for money, "talent," which indicates that possession and ability somehow go hand in hand, not in the
Calvinist sense that wealth is a sign of election, but in
the sense that those with any kind of talent are richer
when they know themselves to be caretakers of their
ability, and poorer when they suppose themselves to be
landlords. "Noblesse oblige" can be saved from a patronizing smugness by knowing that the obligation is
more exacting than any inherited status. If we reign by
gift or genius, we rule by sweat, as Thomas Edison knew
from experience when he said that genius is 1% inspiration and 99% perspiration.

The judgement of Christ took sweat, and happened
on the cross. His judgement sceptre is the rod once used
to beat him: "Vengeance is mine; I will repay, says the
Lord." (*Deut. 32:35;*see also *Rom. 12:19*) Because of the
work involved, the vengeance is a satisfaction far more
joyful than the experience of retaliation. Christ the
Avenger is such in a moral degree, for he restores order,
called the Kingdom, to the operation of grace by letting

himself "perish" instead of the whole Kingdom. If much is required of him to whom much is given, everything is required of him to whom everything is given. A paperhanger endures a stiff neck in order to wallpaper a living room; Michelangelo, with more complaint, nearly breaks his back to paint Christ on the Vicar of Christ's ceiling. Christ bears far more, and does it silently, while he rebuilds the moral fabric of creation.

In the reordered creation, Christ reigns but he needs creatures to rule. He judges men and women according to the presence in them of the interior pride which doubts he can be much of a ruler. For if he is a poor king, then we are poor subjects of the king; but if he is the King of Glory, then we are that glory. At the same time that he inflicts his vengeance on all who will not believe, he will come "to be glorified in his saints, and to be marveled at in all who have believed . . ." (*2 Thess. 1:10*)

The Parable of the Talents describes, then, a sublime banking system which would bring ruin to a selfish economy. There it would only provoke egoism, the most devastating kind of inflation. The ego so inflated is what makes vanity exactly what the word indicates; it gives the impression that we are worthless except for flesh and bones and brain chemistry and cash on account. Human vanity is an appendage to the vanity listed in the third commandment; because we are children of God, to take our name in vain is a judgement against him. On the other hand, according to the parable, we can make a fortune if we know the rate of exchange. The only commodity is the gift of life, the proper exploitation of which comes after rejecting self-doubt, laziness, and fear of criticism. These are the maliciously seductive misjudgements of pride. The humble soul knows its worth; humility becomes the gold standard of the golden rule. In their self-humiliation through vanity, the proud think they are only ego and ultimately worthless, while the humble know that they are the I standing before the countenance of the Thou and thus worth everything.

In the Parables of the Days of Noah and Lot, (*Luke 17:26-30*) another kind of judgement is passed. While the soul is obliged to exploit the potential of the good, it is commensurately bound to counter the potential of the evil. The language used here is qualified and quite inadequate to describe the enormity of evil's vacuousness. Evil's one strength is the weakness of its victim, and its destructive effect is realized when complacency gives it berth. Here lies the ground of human culpability.

The soul cannot afford to relax in the presence of evil; relaxation is just what the word indicates: a return to the passivity of Adam who, having been given authority over all living creatures, relinquished the exercise of that power to Powerlessness. No longer might the Lion lie down with the Lamb; the order of authority has been replaced with a new order in which the shadow of Adam has consumed Adam, making him utterly "a shadow of his former self." He-who-was-Authority is now He-who-is-Complacency. The Garden of Delights becomes a Garden of Illusion since Man, "who walks in a vain shadow," (*Psalm 39:6*) can exist only as a negation and his every exercise of memory is a contradiction of remembering, a dismembering of the power that was in him.

Everything falls when light falls. In the night the shadow is everything, so that nothing can live without living off something else, the Lion off the Lamb, the fire off the wood, the pride off the intellect, the Devil off the Man. If any man were capable of a pure human act then, of course, he would not have to devour anything else to thrive. Then he would have that autonomy once given to Adam, and he would come to see that to be purely human is the antithesis of being merely human. His autonomy would consist in losing his shadow and existing where there is "no variation or shadow due to change," (*James 1:17*) and where consequently there is neither hunger nor thirst nor scorching by the sun or any heat. That requires a different Adam, a new Adam who can walk in the light and who is incapable of walking in a shadow. Such could never be, unless the Light himself were to do it; and such is what he did. And the darkness "has not comprehended it." (*John 1:5*)

A remarkable thing is seen in that light: the Lion and the Lamb not only lie down together, they are the same, just as strength and innocence in such a bright world are the same. Individuality is not lost: the lamb is more the lamb when innocence has a strength of its own and the lion is more the lion when strength has an innocence proper to it. The phenomenon affects everything in the Eternal City. There is neither sun nor moon, for where there are no shadows, neither are there reflections. The account is hardly a fantasy, for fantasies are illusions and there can be no illusions where there are no reflections. And, we can add, where there are no reflections there is no evil, though that can only happen when old Adam loses his self-negation, that shadow which has been his burden since paradise was lost. Inasmuch as man is that old Adam, the goodness of the intellect lets him know that he can only relinquish the burden by "putting on the armour of light." (*Romans 13:12*) He can manage to do that by overcoming the inherited proclivity for sitting in the dark, an inheritance which is, technically speaking, "original sin." Otherwise his case will be that of the lazy man in the tale who missed the sunset because his rocking chair was facing the other way.

The moral significance lies in the fact that such vain disquiet is not done to us but by us. That is the judgement of Noah and Lot whose crime of complacency brought its own sentence. Every instance of modern man railing against what he calls the absurdity of evil remains absurd itself until he acknowledges a human embarrassment. What appears absurd is the logical result of what happens when humans cast to the devils the power which God has given them to cast devils out. When God seems too silent, it is only in those moments when, in his infinite compassion, he wants creation to hear the growl of the beast.

The selfishness for which the soul is judged in the Parable of the Evil Servant (*Luke 19:11*) speaks for itself, but it is a voice growing fainter. A society vague about Christian belief finds the evil of selfishness a difficult concept in spite of its remnant morality. The modern age did not discover selfishness, but it did discover that selfishness might be worshipped. The Master Race, the Parents of the Perfect Baby, and the Me Generation worship at the same altar; Nietzche, the leaders of Planned Parenthood, and the editors of the pop psychology magazines are commonly devout acolytes; and the hymns to romantic genius flow from the rock balladeer's guitar with the same enthusiasm, if not ornamentation, of the "Eroica."

The wicked servant of whom Christ is the Judge is quite convinced that judgement is a single event. Having passed the momentary test, the judged tries to be the judge, "the measure of all things," *Homo homini Deus est*. To the servant's way of thinking, if that which is measured does not fit the egoist's ideal, it can be pounded into shape. Once the ego becomes the ideal it proceeds to become an idol. The blasphemy of idols is not that they are statues but that they are moulds. In the downward spiral of the human consciousness, an impression of reality has replaced the tradition of reality itself. The moral theologian has known all along that this is not a new phenomenon. The proud soul is innately an impressionable soul; and not to belabor the point, passing judgement so far as the proud are concerned consists in little more than making a good impression. Vanity feeds on the vapor of ignorance, like an orchid living on air; the ignorance is the new generation's nearly total historical illiteracy and, unless tutored soon, its scribble will spell social disaster.

In a small corner of the evil servant's story rests an allegory of biological determinism, for if the worship of the self has any ethic it is impurely and complexly that "might makes right." The act of the servant beating the poor underling conforms to the élan of Bonaparte snatching his crown from papal fingers, that "self-realization" is the only salvation. The western democrat has faulted tyrants for many things, but not for wrestling their imperium from the hands of God's judges. The secular sponge has so much soaked up the arrogation that it has become the gospel of much positivist theosophy. That "feel-good" meretriciousness is basically the substance of some media evangelists who, for one reason or another, muddle inchoate religious instincts with the Christian gospel. What happened to the devotees of Nietzsche could happen to the less dramatic attenders of psychiatric clergymen. Banality can be evil since evil is banal. The social positivists' temples may collapse on the coiffured heads of the "Me Generation" as defini-

tively as the Reichstaag fell on the helmeted heads of
the Übermensch. Though undoubtedly, the wall-to-wall
carpeting will cushion the sound.

    While Christ says it is unreasonable to worry about
tomorrow, he also gives us reason to plan for it. Humans
have a certain responsibility, and even an acknowledged
autonomy, in certain aspects of daily affairs. This independence gains its integrity from discerning what it
can and cannot be expected to accomplish. If plaintive
man is not to be Chicken Little screaming that the sky
is falling, in some way he has to share the reliable perspective of those soaring eagles, the Doctors of the
Church, who cry in Greek and Latin and every other
baptized language that the *earth* is falling. At the start
of modern world combat, someone remarked that the
lights were going out all over Europe; it should not have
surprised anyone who remembered that they had gone
out all over Eden.

    The Christian morality calls sin and resurrection from
sin a cosmic event because of the inclusivity of its consequences. Christ expects the Christian to be intelligent
enough to understand that when he speaks of the Bridegroom he is speaking of himself and when he speaks of
bridesmaids, some with lamps burning and some without, he is speaking of the creation around him. Since
that creation keeps going on, the parable can be extended, so that the oil in the lamps is the oil that ran
down the venerable beard of Aaron, on the brow of a
newly crowned king, on a baby at baptism, on the hands
of a priest newly ordained to offer sacrifice for sins, on
the sick asking to be well, and on the dying asking to be
well forever.

There is the ponderous account of the dying Talleyrand who, after having laid aside his episcopal consecration to become a political leader of Rational Man, agreed to receive the last rites of the Church and managed to remember the custom of a priest turning his hands over for anointing, since he has already been anointed once on the palms at ordination. Christ the Judge and Monsieur Talleyrand know the outcome; the parable only says that not all will be invited in by the Bridegroom. Everyone alive harbors the painful recollection of some apostasy against the sovereign order, and each can resolve still to find some oil, light a lamp, and greet the Bridegroom when he appears. Wisdom discerns where the oil is to be found. The universal wisdom of the Church is that this source of light is available wherever the human intellect marks the gulf between self-fulfillment and salvation.

The more the self fills up with self, the less room there is for gladness: an idea odd to anyone for whom the ego is the standard for the definition of value. For the egoist, the bliss in Assisi and Avila can only be the reverberation of psychoneurosis. The psychology of the parable is more astute. The emptiness in lamps which can be filled is what contemporary thought somewhat detachedly calls alienation. Thus the parable of the foolish bridesmaids is a dark comedy of fools; it cannot be a classical tragedy because those who are judged and who have been rejected have no twist of invincible fate to blame for being locked out in the cold. Quite the contrary, they have willfully and imprudently wrapped themselves in themselves.

Christ's sixth ground of judgement concerns the compatible, even necessarily intertwined, qualities of dignity and humor. The Parable of the Sheep and Goats (*Matt. 25:31 ff.*) combines the natural philosophy of every golden age, be it late republican Rome or Elizabethan England, with the celestial revelation given every saint. Horace knew along with St. Clement, and Marlowe along with St. Thomas More, that nothing of substance and worth can be fully enjoyed without dignity and a measure of self-deprecating humor. A model of civilized conduct is the man who dresses for dinner to honor the host and then dresses himself down with an after-dinner joke. Any roast tastes better when you are willing to roast yourself after it. In a way positively hideous to the dilettante and spectacular to the mystic, this is the etiquette of the Heavenly Supper of the Lamb.

Without a sense of occasion, humor becomes silly, and without a sense of humor, dignity becomes pompous. Strike the right balance and you then can strike up a new language with expressions like "Sacred Heart" and "Mystical Banquet" and "Lamb of God." Here is the pattern of the feast grasped for every time a party is held on earth. But each temporal fête is bound to smack of either the Mad Hatter's Party or the obligatory Retirement Banquet, unless the celebrants wash their faces at least once a week to reflect the shine of the Eucharist. The holy Mass is the most important meal in time because it is the only meal gotten from outside time; and it is the feast of Christ only because it is the fast of Satan, prince of pomposity and vulgarity. His deadly crime was to initiate a detachment from the moral harmony in which every soul perceives itself in God's image. The goats of the parable, representing the destruction of worth and humility, do not recognize a *divine* hunger and thirst in every human hunger and thirst. The sheep know that everyone cared for in prison is the presence of God who was made a prisoner to free sinners from sin.

In short, the sixth judgement is against those who do not recognize their ability to be sanctified, and this is so because to help others as "brothers and sisters" and not as "them and us" is to transform a burdensome dialectic into a feast. To see Christ in friends around the table is, in a way which must drive Satan from his habitual equipoise into a dark fury, to declare that Christ inhabits us, too. One expects, and not from wishful thinking since St. John saw it in fact, that there will be no seating confusion at the Heavenly Banquet; heaven will provide the first occasion when the guests can read their names without difficulty. That is the case when, at the feast, human dignity is God's glory and human wit is God's wisdom and, as could hardly be dreamt on earth, man shall see his meaning. The way Christ judges is the way petrified by the sculptors who carved the Last Judgement on cathedral porches; from one side he looks harsh and from the other side he can be nothing other than gentle, but from every angle he is grace. The merely polite will think that duplicit; those who let grace in will have understood it all along.

To pass the test of the parables is not in itself to pass the Final Judgement. A danger remains of doing good; and doing good can be a treacherous thing. God has much forgiveness for the sinner and many rewards for the holy, but there is little if any Scriptural approbation for the kind of individual who goes about "doing" good for goodness' sake. Heaven is not reached by altruism.

Even if we could find some Scriptural support for the "deeds not creeds" sloganeering, it would not change the common aversion to the "do gooder." Children may agree on nothing else in human conduct but they commonly detest the little child whose clothes are the neatest and who gets all the gold stars in school. The short story writer, Saki, had her eaten by a lion in one of his tales. When the end of goodness is misperceived, virtue becomes not a delight but a revenge. Congeniality like that sharpens the art of malice. The individual who is not lazy or complacent or selfish or procrastinating or coarse or humorless is likely to become a tyrant if he does not become a saint.

We are dealing with a primary matter. Goodness must be judged vividly, according to bright beauty and truth. As in the spectrum of primary colors, nothing is complected grey or beige in the judgement of heaven. St. Paul stood in several judgement halls during his earthly sojourn and knew, as does the casuist, that nothing is black and white, either. But unlike the casuist who therefore concludes that the moral element is dull to discern, the Apostle knew it was brilliant. In fact it has only one source and one reference, brilliancy itself:

> If I speak in the tongues of men and of angels, but have not love, I am a noisy gong or a clanging cymbal. And if I have prophetic powers, and understand all mysteries and all knowledge, and if I have all faith, so as to remove mountains, but have not love, I am nothing. If I give away all I have, and if I deliver my body to be burned, but have not love, I gain nothing. (1 Cor. 13:1-3)

As love is the determining principle in judgement, judgement is a reality far more consequential than approval. After all, God created man for delight and out of no obligation to a moral economy. In some mysterious way so lovely that only the innocent young and mature genius can become intimations of it without becoming saccharine, judgement has passed from approbation by judgement to union with the Judge. So Bernanos repeated, "All is grace," and the Judge declares doubly: "God has not sent his Son into the world to judge the world, but so that the world through him might be saved" (*John 3:17*) and, "I have not come to judge the world but to save it. He who rejects me and does not receive my sayings has a judge; the word that I have spoken will be his judge on the last day." (*John 12:47-48*)

Holiness more profound than mere goodness is the counsel here. Goodness as an end in itself is like map reading with no place to go; to miss the subtlety is to become a philanthropist, which is a problem when the philanthropist is not also a saint; in the moral order it is the equivalent of meaning "best" and only saying "goodest." Now "goodest" is child's talk, which is much different from being childlike. Our Lord commanded that a man be childlike to get to heaven; that is the model state of innocence. As such it is the antithesis of childishness which is the deportment of every wrong thinker after the order of the fifth century British monk Pelagius. He thought we could, morally speaking, pull ourselves up by our own bootstraps. The shrewdness of innocence lies, to the contrary, in its refusal to place too much trust in goodness. This does not mean that it dispenses with the moral act; it is just that the innocent have a potential *for* goodness precisely because they do not overestimate the potential *of* goodness. So Christ says that "no one is good" save the Father, and that we should seek first not goodness but the Kingdom and its righteousness and then, and presumably *only* then, will "all else be added." (*Matt. 19:17; Mark 10:18; Matt. 6:33*)

While God certainly enjoins the doing of good (*Rom. 13:3*), the moralizer is easily scandalized that this even needs to be said. St. Paul was determined that it needed saying because he was more than a moralizer; he was positively a moralist, and he recognized that tantamount to bribery is the exhibition of good *things* instead of the Good when standing in front of a judge. If the poor in spirit are the inheritors of the Kingdom it is primarily because they have nothing to offer the judge but themselves. When Christ commended the doing of good works, the purpose was evangelistic, to reveal the Good behind the goodness as the remedy for meanness: "Let your light so shine before men, that they may see your good works and give glory to your Father who is in heaven." (*Matt. 5:16*) Thus there is not the slightest intimation of contradiction when he tells us to be perfect while saying no one is good. (*Luke 18:19; Matt. 5:48*) In a bewilderingly wonderful way, one does not try to be good and build up to perfection; we become perfect and then do good. Or more accurately, we give God permission to be perfect in the soul.

The contrast between goodness and perfection (holiness), between philanthropy and sanctity, is rather like that between a draftsman's circle drawn by compass and the circle Giotto could draw freehand. But how can we draw a perfect circle? That question has taken the form of oratorios and prayers, inquisitions and aspirations, and the sigh of Pilate staring at a blank wall beyond a manacled man: "What is truth?" Pilate's treason against the intellect was the way he turned an interrogation into an apostrophe. The rich young man who asked the Nazarene what he should do to be saved expected an answer. But his outcome was no happier than Pilate's; like Pilate, who knew that Christ was good, and who was corroborated in that by his wife, the rich young man did not notice that Christ was good only because he was the Good. Christ's challenge to them, which abashed their moralizing, was to try and do good from within the Good himself.

Unless this is understood, anyone would think that Christ was passing judgement against the rich when he said it is easier for a camel to go through the eye of a needle than for a rich man to enter the kingdom of heaven. (*Luke 18:25*) He was indicting the reliance on draftmanship instead of art, the compass rather than the free hand, works over grace, the persistent reliance on natural virtue without the infused virtues of faith, hope and love. The fact often overlooked is that he claimed a camel might very well pass through a needle's eye, for "all things are possible with God." It would require, though, that God determine the size of the needle. The Good himself makes the law, and it is far more prudent to follow the law of the Good than to be occupied with the good of the Law.

Capable as it is of considering its own resources, the intellect cannot expect to be its own adequate judge. If nothing else corrupts the case, envy will. St. Paul sought the higher reference of Roman appeal in his own trial, for he knew that Roman law was the fairest he could expect. It remains a monument of disinterested jurisprudence. But the linear dimension of trial by jury or honest judge, anywhere at anytime, will not be sufficient to measure the moral demand made on the development of our human potential. Awesome as the Second Coming of Christ to Judge the world will be, every sane person has asked for it. This is the appeal of the Maranatha, and the substance of the psalms: "O Lord, hear thou my petition . . ." (*Psalm 17:1*) "Be thou my judge, O Lord . . ." (*Psalm 26:1*) "Give sentence with me, O God . . ." (*Psalm 43:1*) These appeals do not criticize the faculties of earthly judges. They would actually be compromised were they tempted to judge the soul. Their obligation is to evidence, which is a world away from the inscrutability of the soul itself. Each judgement in its proper place is sufficient; with good sense a litigant going before Christ the Judge should want to get baptized, but with the same good sense when he goes before an earthly judge his first concern should be to take a shower.

As Christ walked from one judgement scene to the next, he might have given an impression of reading hearts. On the Jericho road the crowd saw an ungainly man in a tree, but the Lord saw in Zaccheus a man who was as good to life as life had been good to him, and who would give him a dinner. To the Jews the Roman centurion was the official lackey of alien exploiters, but Jesus read in him a blunt and honest man who believed in his own pragmatic heart that if you ask the right man the right way he will get the job done. Then there was the adulterous woman, already judged by the men about to stone her, when Jesus let them leave and passed sentence himself after running his fingers in the sand. The human knowledge of divine equity would be helped greatly if one knew what he actually wrote in that sand. The Ten Commandments? The unutterable name God calls himself in an unbearably beautiful song? We do not know. Whatever it was, words or whatever, it blew away. But its portent was in his using earth for pen and paper, for he wrote with his fingers on the ashes of Paradise. He touched this tablet, the ground from which Adam sprung which now was dry and crumbled; the Gardener touched the old, unrecognizable garden and said, "Do not do it again."

It is hard to think of anything more superficial than the idea that he was giving the woman permission to escape. The woman could not escape, at least not into innocence; that was a blocked memory to her. Nor could she escape into guiltlessness; the whole town knew she was guilty. The judgement was one of forgiveness, and that kind of judgement is empowered from heaven. The social utopian probably knows, when pressed for an answer, that he cannot forgive a fallen nature, so he is obliged to deny the fall. Normal people, we said, shrink from the "do-gooder;" and in like manner they dislike the "bleeding-heart" who makes irrational judgements of guiltlessness.

The world has been shown one heart free of that cant; the Sacred Heart does indeed empathize, but both blood and water proceed from it in an exquisite pragmatism which also purifies. To the chagrin of the escapist, this union of heart and the disheartened involves the forgiven soul with an obligation to holiness far more demanding than any agreement to decent conduct. The Sacred Heart, then, judges the soul by nothing so temporal as its obedience to the law; in his magnificent respect for the soul's high dignity, the Heart of Christ judges the soul rather by its likeness to its own love. His judgement is less in what he utters and more in his presence; the confrontation is judgement itself, and not the initiation of it. In the twelfth century St. Bernard said for all centuries: "There are three distinct comings of the Lord of which I know; his coming to men, his coming into men, his coming against men."

It may be hard to believe, outside the persistent sensation of bothersome guilt, that God will judge man in
any discernable way. This itself does not deny that there
can be the transaction of judgement between God and
the human race; such a denial would be a judgement,
if not of God against man, certainly of man against God.
One of the awkward evidences, as well as indictments,
of the existence of a conscious soul is the propensity to
pass judgement on our Creator. A Scotswoman is said
to have complained to her parish minister that someone
had profaned the Sabbath; he reminded her that Christ
himself had violated the Sabbath law more than once.
Her response: "I know. And two wrongs don't make a
right."

The astringent experience of Calvinist rectitude obtained in Judah of the first century, too, as the Gospel
amply shows, and it lives wherever anyone tries to judge
the great Rabbi in trial by jury: "He was a religious
genius; he was a fanatic. He was too ethereal; he was too
earthy. He was too demanding; he was too indulgent."
Even a jury knows that if a deaf man says you are too
softspoken and a man with a hangover says you are too
loud, you probably are speaking the way you should; or
when an Hawaiian and an Eskimo agree that the climate
is eccentric, they are both referring to the four seasons.

When Christ the Judge, then, is judged too spiritual
by the pragmatist and too common by the aesthete, and
when his Church is a gossamer of saints in one novel
and a puzzle palace of corruption in another, it could
signify that the possibility of perfection which Aristotle
located in the intellect has also displayed itself in history.
This does not mean any middling balance between ex-
tremes, "neither up nor down," but the concentration
of all probabilities in one certitude. For every modest

attempt to describe Jesus Christ as the line down the middle of the road which one crosses at one's own peril, there is some historical evidence for maintaining that he has continued to be the Road itself; each time someone urges him to "teach the way," or is satisfied to talk with him "by the way," he replies, "I am the Way." (*John 14:6; see also Luke 20:21, 24:32*) Understandably enough, then, Saint Catherine of Siena said that, if we follow Christ, "all the way to Heaven is Heaven." That, and only really that, is why anyone should feel free to call his judgement right.

Whenever Christ is judged, he turns out to be the judge in what we might call a reciprocity of initiatives. Consider the scene in the Judgement Hall. Pilate, who in his own milieu was as dedicated and worthy as the Pharisees, sincerely wanted to judge Jesus in a way suitable to human dignity and to the apex of that dignity as it was enshrined in Roman law. However, he was a creature of his own commitments; his weakness was the primacy of place he gave to justifying justice. That incontestably perverts the order of justice as it places the prosecution on the defense. Within seconds after Pilate moves the confrontation from the balcony overlooking a lynch mob, he is defensive: "Am I a Jew?" (*John 18:35*) And when Pilate questions, "Are you a king?" Christ makes it sound like an acquittal: "You say that I am." (*John 18:37*)

Christ had maintained that according to perfect law the Sabbath had been made for man, and indeed by inference so was the whole legal system. He could reverse the questions in his own interest, for he was only giving testimony to the truth. "Everyone that is of the truth hears my voice." (*John 18:37*) Then the exasperated sigh of Pilate, which lacks the cavernous and arch-

ing volume of Christ's breath at the tomb of Lazarus,
since it will revivify no one; nor has it the horrible depth
of the last shout from the cross, for it consummates
nothing. If it is to be anything, it is the summation of
uselessness in an arithmetic that adds up to nothing:
"What is truth?" And packing his tattered bag of philosophies, Pilate distractedly moves past the only one
who could have told him. The one reason, if there is any
reason, for hiding behind the pillars and taking in the
scene with its heavy exchange, is that it can happen
again, this time to us, on the Day of Judgement. And
if we sigh as Pilate sighed, the face of the water upon
which the Spirit of God first moved will be hurt, and the
light which heard the first "Fiat" will be hurt, and the
firmament which felt the first division will be hurt; but
most deeply hurt will be the Prince of Truth as he
watches a Lie go by.

There was another figure much like Pilate, save in
externals. Peter was calloused and rough around the
edges but interiorly as practical, decent, and impetuous
as Pilate. But after Peter denied knowing his Master and
was judged by a silent stare, he did not wash his hands,
for his face was bathed in remorse. Pilate was con-
demned by his indifference to man for whom the Law
is given, while Peter was saved by his inextricable commitment to that Love which gave the Law to correct the
"hardness" of the heart. The Law behind the laws knows
that love and hate since they are passions, are cousins.
But between the two lies an alien which is their common
opposite. It is disdain, and this is the human act drained
of will and therefore rendered inhuman. As a result, if
we wash our hands of responsibility, we wash away our
souls. Neither the hot bath nor the cold shower hurt
quite like the basin of tepid water. We are, as the truth

comes to be known, half fire and half ice, with half the scream of the Banshee and half the chant of the Siren, lulling the unwilling intellect into the supposition that there is no human choice, no ground of volition, beyond the apathetic conscience: "I know your works; you are neither cold nor hot. Would that you were cold or hot! So, because you are lukewarm, and neither cold nor hot, I will spew you out of my mouth." (*Rev. 3:15-16*)

The capacity for justice is a capacity for God, and this in turn is what decides our capacity for human acts. Indeed, it decides our capacity for being human at all since we distinguish it from simple animal nature by the evidence of conscience and will. Moral indifference, the tepidity of justice, afflicts the conscience and will in three ways.

The first is an increasing paralysis of the intellect. Facile commitment to impressions replaces the more challenging commitment to objective truth. "I feel" replaces "I think" in the language of the classroom. Then, like dominoes, the syntax of erudition starts a chain of collapse: "I don't understand" falls against "I don't know" and "I don't know" falls against "I disagree," and as these venerable pieces of epistemology are knocked down, a new language arises, spoken as portentously as iambic Latin in gothic Paris: "That's not where I'm coming from" and "Like I mean, you know" and "I'm uncomfortable with that." Eventually, and with social consequences difficult to predict, objective truth will spew this out of its mouth; but for the moment it seems convincing to many that where once *cogito ergo sum*, it now suffices that *sum ergo cogito*. What is this really but an intrusion of pride into the intellectual order where

it finds so convenient a home? It can live there slug-
gishly, not realizing that it is "wretched and miserable
and poor and blind and naked," and can die slowly like
a frog in water heated degree by degree without knowing what is happening. The Italian Theatine, Lorenzo
Scupoli, wrote in the sixteenth century, "If the understanding, the searchlight of the soul, which alone can
discover and rectify the vanity of the heart, is itself
blinded and swollen with pride, who is able to cure it?"
Or as the Book of Proverbs (*14:12*) avers, "There is a
way which seems just to man, but the ends thereof lead
to death."

The chief characteristic of morbid judgement is the
excruciating passivity of the senses, which fail to objec-
tify experience in order to evaluate it reliably. Conscience diminishes, and then will weakens. That which was
human exists as a shade, now only half human in the
sense that it is willing to believe that it has no will of its
own, and claiming no culpability for sin out of the belief
that it is a moral creation of circumstance. On examination, this is just the opposite of liberation; not to be
culpable for anything is a seductive way to say we are
not capable of anything. Inevitably, the soul is held to
account for the wrong idea; a passive will is the result
of a passive conscience. Before we know what is happening, the ego seduced into passivity can see neither
the mountain of ice nor the sea of flame, both of which
motivate the timeless evidences of genius. Then the self
leaves all other commitments to the moral hierarchy and
bathes languorously in that slough of despondency
which it was taught to call the brave new world.

To the degree that it allows itself to become so slug-
gish, the mind has become one of the problems it was
meant to solve. The present generation does not ade-

quately question the oddity of having more psychologists
than philosophers, and paying them more. Logically, it
is as disproportionate as having more cobblers than pe-
destrians. But in the absence of logic, the contemporary
defense only questions the motive for raising the question.

This is as peculiar as the way western democracy fell
rapturously for the progressivist approach to education,
which placed a higher value on the impression of psychological contentment, or "growth," than it placed on
objective learning skills. Then began to express surprise
that the experiment has produced a rate of functional
illiteracy which threatens the national security, not to
mention the viability of an entire culture. In fact, one
inventive apologist for the progressive school volun-
teered the theory that poor testing scores in some public
school systems are the result of radioactive fallout; the
source was unable to explain why the radiation had not
fallen on Catholic schools and other institutions which
use a classical pedagogy. The old question, "Why can't
Johnny read?" has become "Why can't Johnny think?"
and the educators who sowed the seeds often compound
their irresponsibility by refusing to recognize their mistakes. But the enormity is too great for any excuse. Asking the experts who have numbed the intellectual faculty
of a generation if they regret what they did is as useless
as inviting the ancient taskmasters of Sardinia to apol-
ogize to the mineworkers they blinded.

The second affliction endured as a result of a timid
capacity for justice is the sheer inability to be honest.
There is plenty of evidence for this in the widespread
substitution of *ad hominem* refutations for objective dis-

course, debating the person instead of the issue. In the moral order, this ushers in the reign of the euphemism. Any verbal subterfuge, being a detour around the truth, is an apparatus in the etymology of sin. Instead of avoiding the fact of sinfulness, the unfettered euphemism highlights it because sin itself is the great evasion, the flight nowhere.

The word for sin which the New Testament uses, *hamartia*, indicates a missing of the target; and Thucydides specifically used it to signify a wrong turn in the road. Blithe talk of open marriage, assertiveness training, free thought and alternate life styles distract the conscience from admitting that the realities are adultery, selfishness, secularism and perversity. A truth-in-packaging ordinance is needed for the moral order as much as it is in any commercial endeavor. In a consumer society in which the automobile is an extension of one's self, according to some psychiatrists, the intolerable thought of buying a used car is eased by calling it "previously owned." The same slight of speech in moral considerations says there may be vitality in the cast-off bones of weary idealism.

Christ's insistence on perfection, the ground of the Christian's commitment to chastity, is directed toward that honesty which sin beclouds. Free of detours, then, is this "straight and narrow way" which he says leads to his Kingdom. In this connection, honesty also requires that Puritanism not be allowed to discredit purity. An object is not unworthy for having been made a fetish, and the magnificent purity of the saints, functional in its strength and single-mindedness, is not to be despised for the way it is misportrayed by the Puritan. The Sybarite and the Puritan alike are fetishists, one of impurity and the other of purity. The Sybarite is diverted by the bather and the Puritan by the bath; but they are diverted nonetheless, and inasmuch as that is *hamartia* it is not honest. Origen wrote in the first half of the third century:

> Consider that man's heart is no small thing, for it can embrace so much. Do not measure its greatness by its physical dimensions, but by the power of its thought, whereby it is able to attain the knowledge of so many truths. In the heart it is possible to prepare the way of the Lord, to lay out a straight path where the Word and the Wisdom of God may pass. With your honorable conduct and your irreproachable deeds, prepare the Lord's way, smooth out his path so that the Word of God may act in you without hindrance and give you the knowledge of his mysteries and of his coming. (*PG 13, 1856*)

Because Catholic sacramentalism, and not puritanical dualism, is the effective antithesis of impurity, St. John Chrysostom was justified in calling chastity the only virtue needed in order to see God. This does not replace the life of the virtues; it puts them together, rather as one would say a spectrum is the only light needed to see color. Looking around at the daily conduct of mature people, a terrible confusion has settled in as this view of chastity becomes less understood, and it shows itself, oddly enough, in manners. Dress and dialect are superficial concerns in normal estimation; that means they are important. Indeed, next to profound matters, superficial ones are the most important of all in the same economy in which visible reality is nearly as important as that which is invisible. A young man may well take an interest in a young woman he notices on the street even if his intellect is unaware that she is a marriageable young woman. Superficially, she is a lone woman as he is a lone man; more profoundly they may be a lonely woman and a lonely man, but the superficial fact about them is hardly a trite fact.

When superficialities are worked upon they can become even more significant. A spontaneous individual does not betray as many secrets as someone highly formal; an inspiration does not bare the soul half so much as an affectation; and pretension can be as positively riveting as tension itself. The discovery of fire makes civilization possible; the invention of fireworks makes it obvious. Artifice is work; artificial things are disordered only when people pretend that they are not deliberate, as is the case when a casual person tries to "make a statement" by being nonchalant. A negligé is attractive as a deliberate negligence, and the wearer realizes that it would look ridiculous worn to the opera, which is why it is not done. Blue jeans are deliberately informal too, but passing fashion has tried to turn them into a statement by wearing them to formal functions, as though absentmindedly; and deliberate absentmindedness is more than ridiculous. There are moments when nonchalance is patronizing, and there are other moments when it reveals a sinister and dehumanizing inability to be artifical the way inspired nature intended.

Casualness has its merits as does casuistry; but they become perverse when they come to mean the same, for then casualness loses its innocence as casuistry loses its astuteness. There is something coy, for instance, about the highly paid celebrities who compose new "folk songs" for populist causes, just as there is a certain naiveté in progressive parents who let their children call them by their first names and then deny them any instruction in a hierarchy of values. They rob nonchalance of its innocence, and at the same time they manage to turn a sophisticated moral casuistry into an untutored situational ethic. The wit was more accurate than some modern functionalists and nihilists when he said that artificiality is the highest form of sincerity. The artifice is only illegitimate when it is insincere, as in the case of the celebrity saying "I'm just one of you," when everyone around knows he would not have to say that if he were.

Artifice becomes insupportable when self-awareness yields to self-consciousness. In that moment, sincerity yields to cynicism. Louis XIV powdering his hair four times a day was far less pretentious than a rock star mussing his hair four times a day. The king did it unabashedly as a man of the people, quite literally such from cradle to grave, the celebrity does it surreptitiously as a man before the people, which he is so long as it is show time.

One of the most sublimely superficial facts about God is that no one accused him of being unkempt when he walked the face of the earth. No one seemed to notice what he looked like at all; at least they did not think it worth recording, the way they did his cousin's derelict look. There were, of course, unearthly occasions, the apocalyptic appearances, which go into detail about his symbolic appearance, rather the way people photograph the opening of parliament. But the appearance of God is like that of royalty, at least in the sense that they are far more newsworthy when they are *not* dressed up. And it is most newsworthy when they are not dressed in anything. Were a monarch to refuse to wear his crown, political observers would call it a significant step in the evolution of the monarchy, something like a populist president making an important speech in a cardigan sweater; but were he brought out into the public square naked it would be taken as a sign of revolution.

These facts seem to have been taken into account by

God when he lived on earth as a man, for he arranged for them to happen to him. If it seems offensive to people who think God should have higher things on his mind, it is possible that we have grown too proud to judge superficial signs according to their accurate value. Yet much Christology lies in knowing that we never knew so much about God as when he clothed himself in flesh; and we never knew quite why he did that until he let that flesh be unclothed on the cross.

He did not have to be that superficial, but he chose to because he was that deep. It may be, indeed we know it was so, that gold and frankincense and myrrh mean much to God because they are so unnecessary. The waste of ointment from an alabaster jar was more productive in the economy of salvation than the prudent philanthropy of the Pharisee. The cynic, for whom all appearance is suspect, rejects the logic of such a value system. It takes a fully integrated human, that is to say a saint, to know that the naked eye sees less than the eye that is "decked with gladness." The logic of that assessment is displayed in the acknowledged Marian apparitions, for example. They consistently indicate a radiant sort of elegance in the Lady, ennobling the spectator instead of patronizing him. It could hardly have been a case of a peasant engaged in self-projection, for then the Lady would have been all the poorer. The people of Lourdes addressed Bernadette simply as "tu," just as she expected them to, and it was not until the Lady spoke in the grotto that the child heard herself called "vous."

If the world is indeed a stage, we cannot possibly be "merely" players; we are entirely players. And if *all* the world is a stage, there is no place for an audience; the actor simply cannot be a spectator. The secularist, having a horizontal view of creation, thinks he is nothing but a spectator, and his whole judgement of reality is based on how well the "others" act. He finds it difficult to be superficial enough to join the play. The saint is exactly the opposite, participating in "all the world;" and it would seem very dubious to the saint to suggest that anyone can "act natural." Everyone should of course "be natural," but that can be accomplished only by dispensing with modesty. The secularist obstinately refuses. He is like Adam and Eve in a bright green garden wanting to gaze at Rousseau's animals with their grinning white teeth set in broad sunlit smiles. But Adam and Eve could not do that because the Creator insisted that they be part of the light. Persistent as they were, they left the light and the garden too. In short, they left the stage. So they took on an informality known as spiritual death.

On the other hand, formality, or life, is constantly available; and it is to be had through an honest acting out of externals. A saint, for instance, would never speak of "mere sexes" or "mere fetuses" or "mere corpses" as if they were "mere bit players" in a travelling road show. Why, the saint scandalizes the secular empiricist by decorating each with ceremony and songs as all the great players have always done, because the saint is humble enough to know that this play is prehistoric. But at the same time, the player cast out, and thus become a spectator of the play, trying to "act natural" without perfecting his nature, is cursed with the intolerable weight—a burden from which holy men and women have been freed by their humility—which is the dishonesty of modesty.

In addition to the inability to think clearly and the

inability to behave honestly, tepidity of justice (or wrong judgement) has a third consequence: the inability to worship. Only humans can worship. Humanness, like justice, is the capacity for God. As that capacity diminishes, worship gradually gets clotted up into interminable chatter about God. Preaching becomes preachy, and religious instruction very soon becomes a morose didacticism. The point need not belabor itself; there is plenty of evidence around and it provides sufficient excuse to give up, instead of trying to fix the situation. One instance is the hymnody rampant today, and we can only hope that it soon will become couchant, along with the insipidity which often decks the solemn mysteries of marriage and death. The Song of Solomon will surely outlast the sort of thing you hear at weddings now: "Mike and Sue, today you are celebrating what you mean to each other and we are here to affirm you in it." Its cheeriness does not mitigate its groping propensity for shadowy doctrine. In any case, it disserves the bride and groom who should be reminded that one day when "the secrets of all hearts shall be revealed," they will stand in a new marriage before Christ the Judge.

Lapses into trivial praise betray a minor appreciation of that stupendous fact, and of the equally astonishing fact that Christ as Judge is not cruel, for he is the Truth. This also means he is harsh, for truth is as harsh as a bright light in which there is "neither variableness, nor shadow of turning." (*James 1:17*) Harshness hurts only if it lights up flaws. The faded soul appears good only on a dim day with the light behind. Yet judgement does not show us off to any advantage save that of correct perception; and there is neither sunlight nor moonlight in that place of judgement, and certainly no flattering candlelight, because "the glory of God is its light." (*Rev. 21:23*) So the worship which anyone renders to Christ the Judge must mention these things correctly. All singing need not be about *Dies irae*, but without some holy wrath, any Alleluia is a hearty hooray, the dizzy optimism of an *opera bouffe*. It is not enough to tell the Devil to go jump in the lake; the Church invokes a greater power to cast him into the Lake of Fire.

The people know this, but not all the experts do. There are more second-rate liturgists than first-rate ones, and the most deficient are those who skirt around the transcendent implications of sinners in the presence of the sublime. Just look at the mistranslations and reinterpretations of devotional language in order to trace the effects of this mentality on theology. To invite such liturgists to "do" theology is like asking your haberdasher to take out your appendix. You should not complain that they leave scars; it is a wonder that they leave anything at all.

At the heart of worship lies this realization: if justice without mercy is cruel, mercy without justice is weak. Jesus, who was manifestly neither cruel nor weak, said most explicitly that he had come not to judge the world but to save it. He saves it in a way that does not compromise his autonomy, because by the exercise of free will, the soul has to let him save it.

This is a permission, granted by the humility of God which both allows to us and demands of us the three correlatives of right judgement, or the operation of justice, considered above: thoughtfulness, honesty and worship. Their proper ordering works best when grace infuses the soul with the theological virtues of faith, hope, and that love which emanates from Love himself, who is the sole motive for absolute judgement, and

whose ardor is what makes it possible to mention the
fire of judgement with relief.

   Three figures come to mind in speaking about the
operation of justice and, perhaps not without significance for Western assumptions, they happen to be Slavs.
The first, Aleksandr Solzhenitsyn, told American intellectuals:

> On the way from the Renaissance to our days we have
> enriched our experience, but we have lost the concept
> of a Supreme Complete Entity which used to restrain
> our passions and our irresponsibility. We have placed
> too much hope in political and social reforms, only
> to find out that we were being deprived of our most
> precious possession: our spiritual life. In the East, it
> is destroyed by the dealing and machinations of the
> ruling party. In the West, commercial interests tend
> to suffocate it. This is the real crisis. The split in the
> world is less terrible than the fact that the same disease
> is plaguing its two main sections.

The speech was roundly criticized, in a way which illustrated his thesis. One newspaper editorial said he would
not have spoken thus had he been aware of the United
Way or the Boy Scouts. It was tantamount to maintaining
that neither Tiberius nor Caligula could be as base as
Seutonius claimed, for they lived on lyrical Capri.
   On the same terrain, the second figure, Mother Teresa of Calcutta, told women college graduates that on
their wedding day "the most beautiful thing is to give
a virgin heart, a virgin body, a virgin soul." The response
once again confirmed the split in metaphysical consciousness of which Solzhenitsyn had spoken: the objection was less to Mother Teresa's teaching than it was

to her insistence that the better judgement of the human intellect is only possible when it refers to the perfect judgement of a divine intellect. Since such a moral economy is the one sure warrant for the liberal arts, the first thing to be tossed out in an atheistic pedagogy, as we have seen, is intellectual freedom. The day following the address, true to form, a writer in the college newspaper complained: "Many questioned the appropriateness of the choice of Mother Teresa as Class Day speaker." As the historian of social dialectic should know, every tyranny has begun in the name of an unnamed "many" who, when counted, turned out to be the single vote of an *ego* which has disenfranchised the *Thou*.

The third vicarious judge, the Vicar of the Judge himself, has come closer than anyone since the Scholastic enterprise to systematizing the contradictions between egoism and personalism, and representing their consequences for human value. When he was still a relatively unknown figure in the United States, Karol Wojtyla, Archbishop of Cracow, said in an address delivered to the 1976 Eucharistic Congress in Philadelphia:

> We are now standing in the face of the greatest historical confrontation humanity has gone through. I do not think the wide circle of the American society, or the wide circle of the Christian community, realize this fully. We are now facing the final confrontation between the Church and the anti-church, between the Gospel and the anti-gospel. This confrontation lies within the plans of Divine Providence. It is a trial which the whole Church must take up.

The caution has not been altogether well received even by believers. Under the circumstances, the remarks were made in passing and the implications were not clear. No one could have known what was soon to happen to the speaker. But it was the voice of an acute experience, the expression of a man about to become the first pope born in the Twentieth Century and imbued in a singular war with its vicissitudes. The result is a personalism aware that human value is legitimized by the standard of a divine authority, inflated by self-will and deflated by behaviorism.

The judgements of Solzhenitsyn, Mother Teresa and Pope John Paul II have been criticized widely by a pervasive secularism as being limited in their world-view. This betrays a certain provincialism on the part of the critics; provinces can be large, and views are no less provincial for being widespread. Conversely, a vision is not necessarily limited when it is particularized.

Saint Peter and his successors were given the unique endowment of tradition which makes all the difference between opinion and judgement, between appearance and perception, between gold in the hands of Aaron and gold in the hands of the Magi. So Peter said to the crippled man who was begging for gifts at the Temple gate: "Gold and silver have I none; but that which I have give I unto you: in the name of Jesus Christ of Nazareth, walk!" (*Acts 3:6*) The most potent gift extended to the human race today is that same ability to walk, and as man stands up and begins to do it, the moral truth becomes clearer than the stoutest heart has dared to expect: what humans like to call progress leads beyond inventions and explorations straight into the Judgement Hall.

There will be two judgements. The first will be our own when we die. Of this we have certain intimations. One evidence that we are endowed with the faculty of will, for instance, is the propensity to leave wills and testaments. A cartoon some years ago showed a lawyer reading from the deceased's own handwriting: "And to my nephew Harold who asked me to mention him in my will: Hello there, Harold." Instead of leaving a will of his own, Christ, who came to do the will of his Father, breathed on the apostles, and they became his walking testament.

Because of this inheritance, we have come to understand that Christ the Judge, who judges on behalf of his Father, is also defender of man at the time of judgement. God does not want to lose what he has made. A state of mediation after death is provided in which the wills of the souls in Purgatory, who love God however imperfectly, are brought into harmony with his perfect will. Here justice is satisfied by resolving the punishment for sin. Guilt for sin has already been resolved; the souls in Purgatory are objectively forgiven, and are therefore in a condition of potential beatitude. At the same time they are still objectively responsible for the cosmic consequences of their sins as liabilities against justice, for man does not sin in isolation but against the economy of creation. Judas Maccabaeus offered prayer and drachmas in the belief of post-mortem purgation in the second century before Christ (*2 Macc. 12:41-45*) and the dynamic of retribution in the larger life is touched on, too, in the New Testament (see *Matt. 12:32*).

This first is an intrinsic judgement. Since Christ is the measure of all things, he presides as judge in this intermediary stage precisely by being a standard and not by passing a sentence. In a sense far too simple for human comprehension, he functions in this state as ruler of creation in the very way a measuring stick is a ruler. Life and truth, as they will then be understood, and the ambition for glory, will not be "concepts" invented by enthusiastic imaginations. Rather, these will be the realities toward which all along we have been moving inch by inch, growing in stature by shrinking in haughtiness. It is neither mundane nor mechanical. The state of individual judgement is apart from earthly experience first of all and, secondly, it is not engineered. Nor is it, however, *contrary* to earthly reality and natural cause and effect. Since grace does not destroy nature but perfects it, this state of judgement becomes at one and the same time an event. The fact of judgement melts into the act of judging purpose, and the means of accomplishing that purpose coincide, much as if the ability to tell time and to make up for lost time were to become the same thing.

The length of time in this purgatorial state cannot be estimated because it has a purpose instead of a terminus. In one sense, since a soul would not be admitted to Purgatory were it not intended for heaven, the case is somewhat like stepping onto a bridge: for although it initiates a period of passing to the other side, the bridge itself is, so to speak, "already there." Time in Purgatory is less like the time it takes to cross the bridge to get to the other side, and more like the time it takes for the bridge to reach it. The very use of the word "time" is an indulgence of our limited frame of reference; when we pray for those in Purgatory and for ourselves we secure other than "time off." God indulges with his love that knows no bounds. The Christian's objection to the Deist's concept of God as a distant engineer who set the natural order in an architectonic motion of cause and effect and now remains apart from the consequent operation, is based on what Christ showed God to be in experience. Time does matter in God's universe, but he does not count it. As "we live and move, and have our being" in God (*Acts 17:28*), he *is* time.

Within the interaction between time and the Creator of time, the state of life is a history of living; motions of life are capable of emotions; and survival is a growing which, in the instance of humans, has both a biological peak called maturity, and a spiritual peak called sanctification. The former can be timed; the latter must time itself.

For, inasmuch as a man tends to waste time, God indulges that man with time of God's own. Trying to measure such time is as futile as explaining the difference between eight hours of rapture and eight hours of boredom. One can best explain that the period of judgement between death and resurrection of the body is not a vague slumber. Even less is it the constricting spiral of "getting in touch with myself" and "finding where I'm at" and the other solipsisms which defeat the human potential. Rather, such time is an awakening, a movement of "the desire to go and be with Christ," (*Phil. 1:23*) a conscious awareness of the remaining disparateness between my will and the will of God, and a charging of the power of solace and encouragement which the prayer of the faithful and the sacrifice of the Mass daily provide. The temporary suffering that such awareness entails as an exigency of justice has never been absolutely defined by the Church as a pain of sense or a pain of loss, although the Latin doctors are disposed to think it is both. It can in any event be anticipated mystically before death, as in the account given by St. John of the Cross:

> With such punishment God greatly humbles the soul in order to greatly uplift it later; if God did not arrange for these feelings, once experienced to subside

quickly, the soul would die within a few days . . . These
feelings are sometimes so intense that the soul seems
to perceive hell and its own perdition wide open to
its gaze. These souls are numbered among those who
descend live into hell (Psalm 55:15), for they endure
in this life the purgatory due to be endured in the
next. And so the soul may pass through this state, or
it may not, or it may remain in it only a short time;
for one hour of it in this life is of more avail than
many in the next.

If another name were to be given to Purgatory, it would
be Perception.

As was said, there are two judgements. Following individual judgement will come the social judgement of
the whole world. This belief is a trust in Christ's most
abiding warning, and provides the context of all Christian hope. No one can sing "Alleluia" without shouting
"Maranatha." As the end of the Scriptures shows, this
is the prelude to the great Amen. Three truths obtain
here: that the present world will end; that our bodies
will rise from the dead; that Christ will return in his own
presence, or "Parousia," to pass his final judgement on
all things.

The final judgement is the *definitive crisis*. Understood
in its precise meaning, it signifies the point of determination. Fevers have crises, and so, too, can human
history expect a crisis, because it has had a long fever
which has perdured with remarkably consistent effect
regardless of victim or circumstance. The fever of Bru-
tus lunging at his Caesar can pass on to any angry ald-
erman in a weak moment; the pickpocket on the train
has the same high temperature as Alexander plundering
Persia; a shared sweat attacks the Fascists in Abyssinia

and the bully in the playground. The theologians say the cursed affliction came from a forbidden fruit, and no one has found a better explanation, despite what others may say about the dramatic influences of environment. Some would actually propose that it is no fever in any sense, that what seems to be the temperament of the soul is a synonym for the temper of the times, and that we would be better off to call it a legitimate enthusiasm.

The Scriptural description of the world's final crisis mentions a torrent of noise: signs in the moon and the stars, nations in agony bewildered by the clamor of the ocean and the noise of its waves. It would be tempting, and too facile, to pass this off as meaningless language, unless it is also meaningless to say that the X-1 "broke" the sound "barrier." But if the sound does come from the breaking of its barrier, surely, then—although the thought is almost sickening in prospect—there must be a sound even greater at the breaking into eternity.

You do not have to be, (and from the orthodox Christian viewpoint should not be), a necromancer or spiritualist to appreciate how sounds and states in eternity are portentous beyond the wildest hallucinations. But precisely because they transcend abstract consideration are they sensually perceptible. The senses strain to make sense out of those apocalyptic manifestations: elders in white swaddling clothes, blood as bleach, books eaten rather than read, a lamb who is a lamp, and so on; but they seem positively senseless at first only because they are intended for the senses. If we may coin a word, it is not farfetched, it is "nearfetched." Looked at in terms of worship, this is just another way of saying that sacramentalism, that is, the outward manifestation of interior grace, is the acutest science of the senses.

If, as the learned now claim, a great clamor accom-
panied the beginning of the universe at least eighteen
billion years ago, it will prove to be no more sensual
than the shaking of the earth on Good Friday, and never
so audacious as that faint cracking sound made when
bread, become Christ's timeless body, is broken at the
altar in the Eucharist. There is a moment, ever new and
ever the same, when "those who have ears to hear" perceive how the voice of the mighty Christ in Michelangelo's Last Judgement is also Christ the Good Shepherd
calling to his sheep. The shepherding may fully prove
to be more exacting than the judging; a good shepherd
would, after all, lay down his life for the sheep instead
of being content to secure their grazing rights. Those
who hear the voice of the Good Shepherd will recognize
how Christ, who came into the world to judge, could say
with the same solemn verity, "I judge no man."

The crisis of the last judgement entails no action on
the parts of God or of the sinner, but a contrast of wills.
When the vertical will of God is challenged by the horizontal will of man, the result is a cross. So too was once
the perfect cross the perfect resolution. The forgiveness
which Christ asked on the cross for those, who do not
comprehend the full implications of disobedience to the
will of God, is a judgement with consequences qualified
according to how we receive it. "He who rejects me and
does not accept my words has his judge: the word which
I have spoken will judge him on the last day." (*John
12:48*)

That last day is the end of time, that "telos" or ultimate
bestowal of purpose upon time, which initiates the eternity of bliss. The cosmic last judgement, however, is already implied in the individual freedom accorded each
soul in its ability to accept or reject the forgiveness ob-

tained by the passion. The word "passion" in common usage has come to mean the fever of discontent and that lack of control which is the source of alienation instead of atonement. That is not what we mean. Wholeness of personality needs a whole passion, in its more vital sense of suffering through an event. Compassion, necessary as it is for the moral life, is too vicarious to effect a radical change in the individual soul. A willingness to share the passion itself, which is participation in the suffering of Christ as a confluence of personal desire and heavenly love, is the measure by which we are to be judged worthy, or unworthy, of eternal happiness with the Creator.

Christ promised the twelve apostles twelve judgement thrones when the world is "restored" (*Matt. 19:28*) and St. Paul declared that the saints would judge the angels. (*1 Cor. 6:3*) This, then, is the "glorious liberty of the sons of God," and it only obtains when the human personality awakens to the reality of the glory which it offered to it. The first Christian martyr, Saint Stephen, at the moment of his stoning shouted: "I can see the heavens open and the Son of Man at the right hand of God!" (*Acts 7:56*) Those who judged him covered their ears and thus judged themselves. What to them seemed blasphemy was precisely that, it is true, but for a reason they did not understand: they were in actuality blasphemers by refusing to shout out an Amen to the glory which was being offered to them. "What I tell you in the dark, utter in the light; and what you hear whispered, proclaim upon the housetops. And do not fear those who kill the body but cannot kill the soul; rather fear him who can destroy both soul and body in hell." (*Matt. 10:27-28*)

Citing John Damascene, Thomas Aquinas compared the effect of death on humans to the fall of the angels, both being a separation from the eternal bliss for which we were intended from conception. Yet the angels, free of the restrictions of the flesh, have a greater native liberty than do we, and when they reject God, the fall is final. Satan writhes before Christ in the exorcism scenes with a torture no human mind can bend enough to understand. Our human liberty to reject or accept God is imperfect, unlike the decision of the pure angelic intelligences; we "do not know" perfectly what we are doing, even when we act with a formed conscience. Speculation cannot hope to present a certain explanation, but the evidence of God's love lets us trust that he will provide a last judgement after the individual judgements each of us will undergo. That will give our capacity for love a final chance, free of fear and unblinded by ignorance, to embrace his divine will.

Saint Augustine said that a man fears because something that he loves is in danger. At the last judgement there will be two kinds of fear. The first is the chaos of a soul which loves nothing but itself and which is struck by the possibility of absolute annihilation. The second is the awe of a soul which has come to love God more than itself and which consequently knows that it is guaranteed absolute fulfillment of all for which it was created. The first is a case of wanting to die from dread, and the second, wanting to die from love. This latter fear is a synonym for bliss and bursts from the wonder of knowing that the Judge has carried out on himself the sentence for our disobedience. John Newton recognized in it a very amazing work of grace: " 'Twas grace that taught my heart to fear, And grace my heart relieved."

Years from now and today as well, but for all practical purposes the last day, while crossing the street, or in a

comfortable bed, or by a shattering cataclysm, a hand
will slip into hands of others. Some will pull away from
the hand. Ask them and they will say it is cold. Some
will hold it tightly. Ask them and they will say it is warm.
Such, more than anything, will be the singular and final
judgement toward which the soul and all creation has
been moving from the moment motion began. The one
test is the willingness to hold onto him who holds onto
us, that infinitely simple requirement, attained by contradicting every complication of the will. With a devastating courtesy, which Saint Francis of Assisi named "the
sister of charity by which hatred is extinguished and love
is cherished," he will say to each who keeps a hand with
his: "Well done, thou good and faithful servant. Enter
into the joy of thy Lord." (*Matt. 25:21, 23*)

> God the Omnipotent! King, who ordainest
> Thunder thy clarion, the lightning thy sword;
> Show forth thy pity on high where thou reignest:
> Give to us peace in our time, O Lord.
>
> God the All-merciful! earth hath forsaken
> Thy ways all holy, and slighted thy word;
> Bid not thou thy wrath in its terrors awaken:
> Give to us peace in our time, O Lord.
>
> God the All-righteous One! man hath defied thee;
> Yet to eternity standeth thy word,
> Falsehood and wrong shall not tarry beside thee:
> Give to us peace in our time, O Lord.

God the All-provident! earth by thy chast'ning,
Yet shall to freedom and truth be restored;
Through the thick darkness thy kingdom is hast'ning:
Thou wilt give peace in thy time, O Lord.

Henry Fotheringill Chorley, 1842
John Ellerton, 1870

THREE

HELL

Then I turned to see the voice that was speaking to
me, and on turning I saw seven golden lampstands,
and in the midst of the lampstands one like a son of
man, clothed with a long robe and with a golden girdle
round his breast; his head and his hair were white as
snow; his eyes were like a flame of fire, his feet were
like burnished bronze, refined as in a furnace, and
his voice was like the sound of many waters; in his
right hand he held seven stars, from his mouth issued
a shard two-edged sword, and his face was like the
sun shining in full strength. When I saw him, I fell
at his feet as though dead. But he laid his right hand
upon me, saying, "Fear not, I am the first and the
last, and the living one; I died, and behold, I am alive
for evermore, and I have the keys of Death and Hell.
(*Rev. 1:12-18*)

Language about Hell is contentious, and perhaps
more so for the believer than the unbeliever. Unbelief
is willing to tolerate absurdity, and expects it in religion;

but faith in God requires a trust in his benign purpose, and Hell seems an affront to all that such trust implies. Is there then a Hell? And if there is, how can God be good? The second question assumes some answer to the first. But since it is not permissible to assume anything in a secular age except secularity, we proceed to the evidence.

Does Hell exist? The question is in fact more appropriate than asking whether Heaven exists. Hell, as the orthodox believer understands, is derivative, not a part of God's original plan. If it is a place or a state, it is the alternative to that place or state known as Heaven, which God willed. Heaven is where God is; it does not come from anywhere, nor is it an alternative to anything. It "ists" just as Hell "exists." But is this no more than metaphysical poetry?

Were it a symbol, and nothing other, the Church would be more skeptical about Heaven, as she is of all projections, than are the materialist philosophers. There are aspects of Catholic theology which are sharp, and even shocking, in their clinical objectivity. The orthodox theologian, for example, would stolidly turn from the atheist's emotional cry that the goodness of God is contradicted by the horror of a suffering child. He would show even more clinical detachment when scandalized crowds shout that an earthquake has crushed the omniscience of the Trinity.

No one could reasonably deny that the Twentieth Century has produced more human architects of Hell and more natural evidences of hellishness than any other age. More people have gone up in fire and smoke in modern experience than in the sum of every other epoch. This should not be hushed as we boast with undeniable warrant that over half the books ever written have been published in the last fifty years and more than half the products manufactured since the start of civilization, and more than half the scientific discoveries, have seen the light of day only in our own time. But for every few books published one has been burned, and every cure has been matched by a chemical weapon; for each brilliant mind there has lurked a bent one, and sometimes they have been the same. Mass production of information has become what Shakespeare called "Commodity, the bias of the world." This is what we would call "trendiness," and it used to be the affliction of consumers, but now it guides the policy of major shapers of opinion via the electronic media and the schools. No one is more opinionated than the one who thinks everything is just a matter of opinion. By believing in nothing except disbelief, the skeptic is dogmatic about nothing except that one thing. But since that one thing defines everything, everything is subject to it. When practically nothing is a dogma, practically everyone becomes dogmatic. Unbelief refuses to burn a heretic, not because it is humane but because it is absorbed in burning a world. The Twentieth Century is one fleeting example.

Is this evidence of a real Hell, or just of a hellish sense? Hell means an actual state, or even an actual place, of endless ill will and pain, a condition or region in which malice is the only thought and maliciousness the single terrain. If one can build sandcastles, does that prove there must be stonecastles, too? The Christian knows there is a Hell for a reason deeper than the natural intimations of it. The one God-Man spoke of it. Hell is mentioned infrequently in the Scriptures, but those references are divine. The concept can scarcely be a dark blot cast by a malcontent redactor onto the golden tapestry of the sparkling Galilean; on the contrary, in some strange way it forms the shadow which adds dimension to the figures and gives substance to the entire work. Any artist knows that the depiction of a scene in relief requires contrast, just as any engineer knows there is not an up without a down. In the supernatural scheme, the light of heaven was meant to be bright without contrast; but the Fall of Man made Heaven look blank without the cast of that dread shadow which outlines what bliss is not.

At least as far as can be determined from the record, Christ usually spoke in a measured and sober way; but at the mention of the difficult things, a sudden intensity could burst out, like embers flashing into flame. "He straightened up," (*John 8:7, 10*) and so he spoke. It cannot be denied that he spoke most fervently about those matters hardest to understand: devils and angels, Heaven and Hell. These were jabs and not innuendoes, with no room for neutral discourse. And troubling as the torrent is, making it too stark and clear to be rendered in the pastels of impressionism, it is also refreshing, though with the kind of refreshment which is administered rather than sought out. When we ask for a warm rinse he splashes us with cold water; and the sudden awakening makes it ever more difficult to believe those who say that the descriptions of spirits and an afterlife are vague accretions to a plain and basic Gospel. Christ "straightened up" for what are his most audacious and pellucid stabs at the somnolent consciences around him, and so they are offensive the way a punch hurts more than a bruise. Anyone may bruise himself, but only a madman punches himself. And if mortal sensibility is bitter, and we are not mad, then this must mean there is someone besides ourselves giving offense.

He is not a Pharisee, nor is he a fisherman or an anonymous face in the crowd. He is one who preached "having authority" (*Matt. 7:29*) because he had seen the things whereof he spoke. His exclamations to human sensibility are never uncontrolled or vindictive, for all their intensity. Rather, we can soon come to see that they are meant to snap the soul out of rancorous posturings. The natural intellect is never quite so out of control, and experience quite so embittered, as when the intellect slips into that fearsome refusal to acknowledge, in its own sphere of seen and unseen presences, the intimation of another sphere which is home to presences even "more" real for being visible and invisible. Each time experience denies this, the soul lapses into a harsh lethargy. Hell and Heaven are thought to be attitudes and figures of speech. No matter what they may incidentally be called, earthly glimpses of them torment the imagination; and this for the simple reason that when all feeling grows numb and grammar disappears, an inescapable voice, which refuses to hush itself into a discourse, shouts Hell and Heaven as it did beside stone cities and sand coasts.

Jesus debated the great moral issues but he proclaimed Hell and Heaven. There would be no exchange of opinion or existential argument on those two subjects, for no one else could know about them. He gave his hearers Hell and he gave them Heaven, and so long as his listeners were earthly, any debate about Heaven and Hell would be shadow boxing. For Jesus spoke with such black and white certitude, even when he opened his mouth in parables for those who were not apostles, that the shadow boxer would have to box the light, too. Just once did that happen, on Good Friday; and with one great blow there flashed a lightning voice to blast the name Heaven all the way to Hell.

Next to Christ himself, no one in the primitive account spoke with deeper certitude than John the Baptist, announcing that the Rabbi from Heaven would "purge his threshing floor" and "gather the wheat into his barn," and burn the chaff "with unquenchable fire." (*Matt. 3:12, Luke 3:17*) The Messiah corroborated the outpouring in parallel metaphor: "In the time of harvest I will say to the reapers, gather together first the tares and bind them in bundles to burn them: but gather the wheat into my barn." (*Matt. 13:30*) Then the unutterable configuration of God breaks through the vestige of allusion: "The Son of man will send his angels, and they will gather out of his kingdom all causes of sin and all evildoers, and throw them into the furnace of fire; there men will weep and gnash their teeth. Then the righteous will shine like the sun in the kingdom of their Father. He who has ears, let him hear." (*Matt. 13:41-43*)

Such writers as Clement of Alexandria, Origen, and even Gregory of Nyssa held that since God is "all in all," there cannot exist an autonomous Hell for all time, that there must eventually be a universal reconciliation between God and even the most heinous and disobedient of his creatures. The exterior congeniality of the idea, sometimes called Universalism and Apocatastasis, attracts similarly expansive people today, from the domestic Moravians to a sophisticate like Graham Greene. Against the beguiling wish, however, persists a disquieting fact which impinges upon us as it did on St. Augustine and the Fathers of the Council of Constantinople: suffering consists not simply of an absence of the good, for Goodness himself felt its unmerciful pain. The merciful Christ anticipated the calamitous meeting of his constructive love with its corrosive enemy, hate. He compared the endless state of this terrible end of mercy to

Gehenna, a trash pit in Jerusalem whose perpetual little pillars of smoke mocked the pillar of the cloud by day and fire by night which had led the Hebrews to the promised land. Smouldering Gehenna was the sign for two factors of Hell: fire and isolation. Additionally, in this vast wasteland of junked creation and ruined mercy, there is "weeping", that is, physical pain which sears the soul instead of enflaming it, and there is "gnashing of teeth," which is the metaphysical torment of anxiety, the last loneliness of a soul deprived of any future and left to an aimless yet ceaseless striving (see *Matt. 8:12; 13:42; 22:13; 24:51; 25:30; Luke 13:28*).

Hell also contains that ghastly condition in which the one illusion left says there is something better than joy, the quest of which is *anxiety*. Anxious, gnashing teeth may seem crude, but crudeness is appropriate in this place; for the soul in Hell has turned its primitiveness inside out in such a way and with such issue that the superstitions of mankind's prehistoric career are now the phantoms of posthistory. The myth of the noble savage free of complaint has its counterpart in the myth of modern man conquering complaint. If all the weeping caused by disease and war could be wiped away by medical science and universal disarmament, the children of Adam would still gnash their teeth about what is yet to be. An indefatigable hellfire-and-damnation preacher is said to have told a toothless sinner that in Hell "teeth will be provided." He has his unlikely supporters in the psychoanalyst and sociologist who appreciate the inventiveness of society when it comes to gnawing at enviable people.

Discontent and false witness provoked by envy can be found at any stage of earthly accomplishment and success; it is a slightly macabre tribute to man's dignity, as it suggests he has a higher source and nobler destiny than he can explain on his own. He is more than a biological riddle which can solve itself by being praised and rewarded by other riddles. The sighs of Midas in his golden mansion and the sobs of Alexander with no more lands to arrest are either the most hideous or holiest of sounds, and the soul can expect to know why only at the end of time, when all is gold and everything is conquered; some call it Hell and some say it is nothing less than Heaven.

"There shall be two [men] in the field. The one shall be taken and the other left. Two women shall be grinding at the mill, the one shall be taken and the other left". (*Matt. 24:40*) Little by little one comes to see that the mystery deepens: the two belong to the same field, to the same mill. The field and the mill are neutral situations, but those in them cannot remain neutral in any plausible sense inasmuch as they are moral creatures: "one shall be taken and the other left." And Hell, upon examination, is the false neutrality which the intelligence is free to choose as the alternative to love. It is the one example of an absolutely autonomous human will.

God's will is absolute and creative, and original sin tethers human will between half obedience and half disobedience to it; but when freed of earthly compromise after death, the moral tether breaks and releases the soul to make one absolute act of the will which can achieve either perfect harmony with divine creativity, or perfect disharmony and diabolic ruin.

Desolation is not a nothingness; in the most perverse enterprise, it is the blatant construction of destruction. The soul that chooses it realizes, too late, that nothing is ultimately neutral in the moral order. "If God is for us, who can be against us?" (*2 Rom. 8:31*) Sin turns this question into a declaration. In Hell, the pronoun Who becomes a name; there, "Who" *is* against us. He lamentably is very much against us, for Who is the hollow name of Satan.

Death is love's contradiction, and Hell is the daunting state of death after death, a post-mortem of the ego, making a soul aware of its self-contradiction and unable to do anything more about it. It is the realization of the ego's dream to live without a super ego; but suddenly the dream becomes a horror as transcendent references keep breaking in on it. Certainly God does not cease being when he is ignored, and so the only way the ego can be without him is to be outside him. Such is spiritual exile, and the Hell of it is the fact that there is no recovery from the loss and no return to the source. So Christ's injunction not to be anxious (*Matt. 6:25-34; Luke 12:22-31*), contains a pragmatism overlooked by the exegetes who think there must be consolations more forthright for real people with real problems than those in his discourse on the lilies of the field: the lilies and Solomon's glory mean that there is more to us than we ourselves. There is no life which will be denied, provided we do not try to live it alone.

Though Hell cannot be proven by unaided natural observation, it can be indicated. For all the frequent talk of a "post-Christian age," culture may be headed for a Christian revitalization without precedent, motivated in part by the contradictions of recent events which have illustrated what can happen when humans reject the root of their humanity. The first House of Hell on earth was Babel and the people thought it was tall. The contemporary age of materialism has fabricated more than a mere symbol of disunion and chaos: the skyscraper has shamefully scratched Heaven by making a Highrise of Hell. The same syndrome which can make a Hell for society can make a Hell out of society; it would hardly be possible to say so-and-so looks like Hell had we no construction experience. The will does not only choose, but can help define the choice: "The mind is its own place, and in itself / Can make a Heaven of Hell, and Hell of Heaven." (*Paradise Lost*)

One may not put it Milton's way, but one inescapably has opportunity to feel it that way. Opportunities abound in hospitals where on the same corridor babies are being born and aborted, nursed and shredded; many had the opportunity in Cambodia as the Pol Pot regime systematically tortured and killed fully a third of the population. In the United States the number of deaths from the silent holocaust of abortion, in the first ten years following the Supreme Court's *Roe* vs. *Wade* decision, had already become ten times greater than the nation's deaths in its wars; and while in terms of proportion to population the Cambodian massacre was the largest in human history, the most people killed at the direction of one man were those more than sixty million estimated to have died under Mao-tse-tung between 1949 and his own death in 1976. Contemporary civilization seems to have lost some of its bequeathed imagination for horror as a result of the way reality has outrun it. But this has a perilous consequence, as it socializes Hell.

It does not take imagination to picture Hell for the very reason that Hell is the state of no imagination. One says almost instinctively that a thing is boring as Hell. The existentialist is egotistical and wrong to think Hell is other people, but he is correct in using boredom as a frame of social reference. George Bernard Shaw came closer to the target: "Hell is a place where you have nothing to do but amuse yourself."

Boredom must be caused. After all, only *people* are capable of it, and unless it is a fickle curse it must be the obverse of some great gift. Certainly the builder-insects seem relentless in their capacity for this boredom: no one has discovered a fed-up ant, a constrained spider, the bored bee. Only people take days off. But it is not altogether clear what the thing is from which the days are being taken.

There is an association between the capacity to create and to recreate. The capacity for recreation is the intuition of a difference between sequence and consequence. A Christian can relate this to the distinction between false Quietism and practical Mysticism. Quietism is an indifferent passivity while Mysticism is a deliberate abandonment which is acquired through acts of virtue. Similarly, the difference concerns the distinction between the collective and the community, and modern man lays the foundation of social Hell by failing to consider how such a distinction obtains. The philosophy of phenomenology tries to figure it out, but can only succeed when it yields to the radical facts of how God made man able to communicate with him and for him. The second chapter of Genesis describes work as the means by which we act out the divine image by being ministers of God in creation. When the individual insists on being without God, and forsakes merit for meretriciousness, labor becomes a heavy sorrow. When work is aimless, workers get bored, because aimlessness is a contradiction of their identity.

God made all things out of nothing. But once having been formed *ex nihilo*, we cannot return *ad nihilum*; indeed, man can only expect to exercise his freedom, given by the donation of the divine image in the soul, to separate himself from that creative process. If it is not pos-

sible to go back to nothing, it is appallingly possible to
collapse into nothingness; and, more than a possibility,
contemporary experience has shown it to be a certainty
whenever confidence in life's purpose is abandoned.
The Fall of Man gave us sin, but this Collapse of Man
has given us an affliction which has come close to wiping
the smile from curiosity. Adam grabbed the fruit of the
forbidden tree of the knowledge of good and evil; but
modern man has lapsed into an actual vacuum of spirit
in which he finds himself too bored to be tempted. Victor
Frankl, freed from the ashes of Auschwitz, based the
third school of Viennese psychiatry, Logotherapy, on
the awesome effects of this sense of meaninglessness.

The Fall differs from the Collapse the way nothing
differs from nothingness; nothing is unaware of itself,
nothingness is aware of nothing else. At least the state
of nothing has some potential: Adam's fall was the *felix
culpa*, the fault which proved to be fortunate from the
retrospective of the Second Adam. But nothingness is
utter inertia, wailing to the deaf, consumption when
there is no chance of consummation. The ghastliness of
the Collapse is not to be found in its void, as there is no
thing there, but in the one faculty remaining to those
who are there: namely, the awareness that they are
where no thing is. Call it a state rather than a spectacle,
for there is nothing to see, and in its perversity this also
means that there is nothing to *be*. At one point a healed
man says of Jesus, "Without God this man could do
nothing." (*John 9:12*) He was making a double statement,
for in the grammar of dissent, or the anxiety of the
damned, it is rendered: "Without God this man could
do nothingness." The free will which chooses to be without God twists its own freedom into this ultimate catas-
trophe.

The Prince of Lies is the Act of Nothingness (and such nothingness, or naught, is the full strength of the Elizabethan word "naughtiness" which modern English weakened into a child's scold). Even as Nothingness, he still is an angel, however fallen. The consequence of this for the definition of Hell is that he cannot fathom his own memory of the good. When he meets Christ, for instance, he cannot stop himself from doing homage and making a tortuous obeisance (see *Mark 5:6*). As the intelligence of Nothingness, he remains a reflection of its opposite which includes Everything. He is then unparalleled, save by the good angels themselves, in his appearance of sparkling attractiveness and mobility and liveliness. One would not probably find him in the gutter, but one would be disposed to invite him to add glitter to a social function. He is the Lord of Darkness precisely, and the lordliness makes him all the more compelling and terrible. This, by the way, is why people interviewed on the news programs say that their next-door neighbor was the last one you would ever expect to axe his wife; he was frequently raising money for charity and playing the clown for children.

There are, however, two traits which betray Satan sooner or later. They are commonly called the characteristics of evil.

The first is a thudding lack of originality. Here the Evil One is more insect-like than human; he can only repeat the same hives and webs from wornout blueprints. There is some clue to the invisible architecture of Hell in Albert Speer's eclectic and numbing schemes for the new Berlin; and, though it may seem retrograde to admit, it is also in the brutalism of Le Corbusier's utilitarian designs for a disemboweled Paris. The repetitiveness of the puritanical International Modern

style, which until the present moment has been the un-
questioned gospel of functionalism in architecture, is
almost identical to the classical symmetry; but, hard as
it is to place a finger on it, the difference cannot be
passed off as a cultural fancy. Neither culture nor anthropology can adequately explain it. But brutalism is
the husk and classicism the core of exuberant creativity.
Both the Fascist and the Bauhaus architects insisted that
they were creative. The warning signal today is the announcement that someone is about to be "creative;" it
is the sure sign of the opposite in an urban society. The
savant can precisely thank God that Maurice de Sully
and Fra Angelico did not set out to be original, for then
there would not be the Cathedral of Notre Dame or
myriads of painted angels. Instead of trying to express
themselves, they tried to copy the expression of God
and, by accomplishing what they had set out to do, they
produced the only authentic originality, a unique re-
production. The alternative, which has tyrannized urban societies for the last couple of generations of
relentless glass boxes and "machines for living," is a re-
produced self-projection, or solipsism.

The architectural problem is a moral problem. While
there is original sin there are no original sins; hence it
frequently has been observed how there are only the
same old sins being tried by new people. Original sin is
a lack, an absence of the original justice which manifests
itself through sanctifying grace and the consequent integrity of will. Sins are momentarily thrilling not because
they are the newest things but because they are the oldest
things; they play Adam instead of Christ. The latest
scandal out of Hollywood is inevitably the earliest sin
out of Eden. And, in the same order, the latest invention
is never other than the most recent means of assisting

the earliest virtue out of Eden, man himself. Yet no one can invent man, for any man can only reproduce. The New Man of modernism is a continued relapse to Old Adam. To be up to date is merely a way to become out of date. Any man can be really new only if he reproduces the intention of God in creation. Without it, he is bound to regress to a debased functionalism.

Any banality should bring the human consciousness to the ramparts of logic in defense against the uninventive illogic of evil. Taking the stand is near to winning the battle. While the Evil One has a clever strategy it is his only one. The Prince of Hell may fascinate and beguile, but if we have read his latest blueprint, which anyone can do by reading the spaces between the lines in the history books, he will never surprise.

Evil's second characteristic is the cruelty implicit in the first. Pleasure can no longer produce satisfaction, because it is tyrannized by tedium. It has to be pursued relentlessly or it will escape. The sensualist has to work hard at indulging himself; he can never give his addiction a rest. There is a definite principle behind this. As the moral law is inverted, the exterior senses absorb the interior senses, so that sensual stimuli replace imagination and inspiration as means of cognition. It is as if the only way to know you have a tooth gets to be by drilling the nerve. Given an eternity of this, as in Hell, the one exterior pleasure which might distract from painful sensuality is the sheer gratuitousness of a painful act inflicted on someone else, an eternal experience of that temporal situation in which couchant lust soon turns its eyes to rampant sadism. Hell is indeed a society; Saint Augustine called it a city and Saint Ignatius a camp. But it reverses the normal pattern of societies forming for the common good and defense. The dark realm allows access between souls solely for the purpose of exploitation and affliction. Were one able to streamline the monstrous while preserving the monstrosity, or to pacify hysteria without abating its disintegration of the faculties, then one would have accomplished the bureaucracy of Hell.

At this point it would be vacuous to say God must be cruel to allow this. The blatant truth is that he neither allows nor disallows it. He perfectly and simply knows what Hell denies. Hell perpetuates itself only by denying itself, rather as a shadow feeds on its own inability to cast a shadow. "Hell does exist, my friends," said the Curé d'Ars, affirming that Hell lacks aseity, or underived being. That is, Hell becomes a sufficient fact only by the act of withdrawing from the blessedness of the One who Is; Hell exists as the Exit. In this mystery, *ex* really does mark the spot. Sartre was mistaken to think Hell has no exit; it is nothing but exits, an enclosure of open doors, a fence made entirely of gates ajar. The curiosity is that there are no walls and, by some hideous arrangement, its inhabitants enter it by taking the way out.

The literalist could criticize any one of these metaphors, if not out of pedantry then surely out of patience, on the grounds that the subject is too important to be merely hinted at. But the Messianic pronouncements give some ground for saying that no one should dare to do anything other than hint. If the glory of Heaven is too great for carnal perception to bear in this present life, the rancor of Hell must weigh unbearably. Dwelling much on Hell could become tantamount to dwelling in it, and a man cannot be so morose and still be faithful to his baptism. Even when he alluded to Hell, Christ's imagery was brighter than the slumber under which the

Pharisees cast the good and bad alike in Sheol, the land
of the living dead. He uses the image of fire for Hell
because there are two kinds of fire. The first purges,
firing crystal, porcelain and steel, and so he baptizes
with the Holy Spirit and with fire. The second kind
destroys. A candle on a stand gives light to the whole
house (see *Matt. 5:15; Mark 4:21; Luke 8:16*), but a candle
knocked off a stand can burn down the whole house.
So it is with the case of an angel knocked out of Heaven,
and the damage done can then be so great that it scarcely
matters whether it comes by fire or ice.

Saint Augustine said there is "no way of waiving or
weakening" the Lord's words about everlasting fire, but
it would be doing exactly that to imagine this fire to be
merely flame. It is endless destruction, devoid of any
potential for purgation. Burned out and frozen out are
equal descriptions of the pain of the reason as it becomes
conscious of irretrievable separation from all faith, all
love and all hope. When the reason is atrophied in such
a state, the will becomes frenetic; the reason is the moth
in the flame, and the will is the moth darting around
the flame, and yet they are the same moth. And such
is the cause of the body's suffering; for our very person,
and not only our soul, or any one element of our identity, is victim of this torment: "It is better for you to
enter into life crippled, than to have two hands and go
to Hell, into the fire that cannot be put out." (*Mark 9:43*)
Utter willfulness can get man into trouble in the next
life just as it can in this. St. Thomas Aquinas said all we
need to do to be saints is to will it; so we can be damned,
too, simply by willing it. Damnation is not the result of
absentmindedness.

By its nature as the corruption of the good, as we have
already seen, evil is anything but absence of the good.

It is certainly a contradiction of the good; but in its own time primeval it wrested from that same good whatever power it now has. An honest paleontology of evil will reach the same conclusion in its disputations as did Jacob wrestling with the angel. It will not be the easy solution of Universalism, saying that there can be no eternal Hell in the justice of a good God; nor will it be Dualism, which attributes to Evil an autonomous power equal to that of the Good. But it will acknowledge the reality of a struggle for the soul to which Evil lays a tenuous claim.

Battle language is more suitable than ethics when talking about salvation. Humans are not defects but rebels, and their salvation consists not in reformation but in enlistment. The Good did not come to earth to make us good; he came to make us perfect, and that takes more than improvement, it takes union with God. Improved eugenics and social reform remain Pyrrhic victories against evil, until they emanate from some cosmic re-alignment of forces which will be effective against the strategems of Evil: "For our wrestling is not against flesh and blood, but against the rulers of the world of this darkness, against the spirits of wickedness." (*Eph. 6:12*) There are angels sent to guard and protect us in the battle because Satan, while not God, is an angel and thus has access to ploys which are more than human. And because he is angelic, he can break hearts so delicately that at the time it may seem thrilling.

A great writer thought the flashing neon signs in Times Square would be beautiful if one could not read them. An illiterate Muslim might see in a Coca Cola sign an arabesque worthy of a mosque. The lettering of Hell can persuade only through illiteracy, too; it is the absolute contradiction of celestial script: "When you see a cloud rising in the west, you say immediately that the

rain is coming—and so it does. When the wind blows
from the south, you say it is going to be hot—and so it
is. You hypocrites! If you can interpret the portents of
earth and sky, why can you not read the signs of the
times?" (*Luke 12:54-56*)

The Ezekiel in Everyman gazes out at what appears
to be a valley beautiful in the moonlight, a gently un-
dulating terrain crisscrossed with elegant shafts of ivory
and ebony bathed in a silvery glow. But the reverie is
broken, as it was for the prophet, by the Word which
intones the real interpretation: "These are the bones of
the house of Israel" (see *Ezekiel 37*). The carnal eye has
difficulty distinguishing the valley of the shadow of
death and the green pastures, the sneer and the smile,
the collective and the family, the corpse and the body,
the manipulator and the consecrator. These reveal
themselves to an interior interpreter; and this is why the
Prince of Hell relentlessly and almost gallantly, wants
to break the heart, for that is the way to blind the soul.
A heart would either have to be immaculately free of
his seduction, or sacredly stronger than it, not to be
blinded to the signs of the times. And so there is a story,
and it is true, which says there actually is a heart with
both such qualities: once on a hill outside the city of the
great King, the Prince of Darkness tried to break the
Heart and both its qualities at the same time, but he only
managed to pierce it. The sky was blinded, but three
days later it saw the light again.

Human vision would attain perfect clarity if it conformed to that interior law of optics which is "purity of
heart." Impurity of vision, which cannot see God, explains our inflated moral economy in which it is so easy
to swindle sensible people into buying acre upon acre
of dry bones. Wrap a bone in all ill-gotten stock certif-

icate and it brings a good price; wrap it in the red flag
of revolution and it looks pretty; piece the driest bones
together into "man come of age" and the gullible will
call anyone who objects "spineless." Toss the crowd
bones called a worker's paradise, a consumer's utopia,
inevitable progress, a great society free of policemen
and priests snapping at your heels, and you will be sur-
rounded by even more to feed. The problem is that
sooner or later the bones will necessarily be discarded,
stacked up once again in the Valley of the Shadow like
splintered shafts in the vacant moonlight. The phenomenon should hardly surprise any reader of Herodotus
or Gibbon or the daily newspaper. *Vox et praeterea nihil.*
The one thing newsworthy about it today is that while
other ages eventually ran out of bones, ours has filled
the valley and still has more bones to bury.

Had Christ been the deceiver, the swindled would
have smashed his body the Church without a moment's
hesitation. But the thieves have consistently been against
the Church and still the thieved attack the Church. A
mind fed up with ugliness will turn ugly against the
House of Beauty. A mind fed full of lies will lie against
the House of Truth. A mind fed sick on evil will wish
evil on the House of Good. The explanation is guilt.
People who buy their way into Hell know it is Hell, and
they cannot bear to have God remind them.

In former times inhumanity justified itself by citing
an enemy. Each crusader had his infidel. The more som-
ber tendency today is to call the enemy a mental defective. God never corrodes our dignity that way; to him
we are a rebellious generation, never a defective one.
But such is not the case when the sense of human dignity
is compromised. Mental asylums in pre-psychiatric times
were little better than prisons; in some societies prisons

for political dissidents are called mental asylums. Evil has a systematized logic which makes sense provided the system is allowed to work backwards. In the Twentieth Century it drew on science to replace the martial screams of Waterloo and the Crimea with recorded symphonic music to entertain the neat columns of silent casualties filing into poison showers. The logic was not civilized, but it was not barbarian either. It was the mental network of men and women who had moved beyond civilization. They called their position a move beyond God, but the two false progresses, beyond civilization and beyond God, are the same essential regress. Transposed from sociology to theology, their claim was not the declaration of belief, nor of unbelief; it was the cold breath of souls grown numb to their Creator.

The transposition marks a transition which is uniquely modern, because it looks upon itself as a pilgrimage. The flight from God has come to be called a march to paradise. The modern pilgrim has called God a vain thing, and then embraces Vanity itself. The teacher Qoholeth railed against the huge Vanity of Vanities (*Eccl. 1:2*), the fatal unfamiliarity with God which breeds self-contempt; but it has taken our own infatuated age to prove its existence through the three teachers of misanthropy: Nietzsche, Marx and Freud. Each, with a different motive and form of expression, concluded that it is useless, and indeed even erroneous, to estimate the human condition with the help of supernatural reference; man is his own measure. They never could gauge the consequences of their attempts to declare the age of post-theism.

While there cannot be an actual age "after God," there can be a post-modern age. It has begun already, as the modern intellectuals lose confidence in their ability to turn social contemporaneity into the religion of modernism based on the sufficiency of temporal phenomenon to provide ultimate truths. The post-modern age began with the realization that any attempt to explain the world by secularizing ourselves is about as effective as trying to improve the eyesight by making a spectacle of ourselves. The truth struck once the practical results of modern assumptions began to be felt. Collectivism, for instance, can no longer be excused as vulgarizations of orthodox modernity. It is the tangible product of a paleo-scientism which weaves the threads of philosophy, economics and psychology into a blanket which all but smothers the human spirit. The old masters of populism cannot complain without impunity that they have been popularized by the people.

Emil Brunner suggested that Hitler, the archetypal man—beyond—God, should posthumously be given an honorary doctorate in divinity for having taught the world what Hell must be like. With Wagnerian music at high pitch, the doctor of dark things celebrated the two great festivals of creation underground in the Berlin bunker. In the last days of his life he celebrated his birthday and marriage according to the inchoate rites of living people already beyond their source. It was a kind of Black Mass, for Evil has no originality, and hence no liturgy of its own, and can therefore only give form to its chaos by being the Eucharist backwards.

Satan, who can do nothingness, can do no new thing, and remains a parasite of the good which God has made. Since he cannot ascend to Heaven, he will take the old hymns of light and sing them darkly below. He abides in an endless awareness of his inability to be annihilated. Damnation is not death, so it turns out, but helplessness to experience the death of death. It is indisputably a living Hell, and it is Hell because it cannot help being alive. Endlessness does to immortality in Hell what Gulliver's comparative smallness did to perception in Brobdingnag, where the beauty marks on the giant women appeared stupendously ugly close up. As for the hymns of Hell, they sound like a needle stuck on a recording of the Hallelujah Chorus. We do not mind a hiccup, but what if we were to hiccup for ten thousand years? So it is with every unrepented sin and each unworthy communion; if they do not save they will magnify until they damn. No rigorist taught that; it comes on the authority of the generous Apostle (see *1 Cor. 11:29*).

Where, then, is the Good Shepherd? Where is the Bridegroom, the Prince of Peace, the King of Love? That is the second question we set out to ask. Are these disguises and is he grinning by the Lake of Fire? If there is truth to the inspiration which has moved the greatest souls to the noblest actions, then there is also truth in saying that the Good Shepherd is weeping on a hill as he sees what is going on. If those who are damned by their own willfulness weep and gnash their teeth, so does the rejected Saviour mourn for them: "Jerusalem! Jerusalem! That killest the prophets and stonest them that were sent unto you. How often would I have gathered you unto me as a hen gathers her chicks, and you would not." (*Matt. 23:37*)

His certitude about the desolation of the city did not provoke any political intervention on his part. The citizens of the city were stamped with his image, and to deny them free will would be to ruin their chance of Heaven as much as of Hell. It was a supernatural version of the decision to sacrifice Coventry in the Second World

War rather than disclose to the enemy that British Intelligence had cracked its code.

No problems would exist without moral freedom, but neither would there be any solutions; and, in a roundabout kind of way, the integrity of the conscience in the final analysis depends less on its security and more on its ability to make itself secure. While it is comforting to have a fireplace, it is more comforting to know how to build a fire.

Any authentic satisfaction requires a certain independence. Dissatisfaction in the most affluent societies, whose demands are based on wants more than needs, indicates that such unhappiness is the tyranny of self-gratification. Unless rewards can be freely chosen or rejected, they become frail tokens of some bondage to the giver of the gifts. The "emptying of God," his *kenosis*, by which God the Son came to earth as a man, was an exposure to the possibility of rejection (see *Phil. 2:7*). The essence of that species of emptying is humility, not hollowness. Rejection, and acceptance, both require humility; otherwise we become possessions. While the proud claim that they want to "pick and choose" and be possessed by no one, the truth is the opposite. Pride is insatiable in its need for gratification; as a result, it cannot discern its needs because it is distracted by wants, and the direst want is not only to be in the world but to be of it.

Pride is thus the antithesis of self-possession, and this paradox marks why the proud, having declared themselves more powerful than anything, can be bought for a medal or a diploma, or even the confidence of a gossip. Pride, then, burlesques the kenotic process; if the soul will not expose itself to rejection, it is certain to be rejected. If it insists on filling itself, it certainly will be hollow. Pride hollows out Hell to the grief of our humble Savior who emptied himself that we might not be empty.

A city boy at summer camp in Vermont was caught in the act of kicking a toad by one of the locals. The boy said, "I can do what I want. He's my toad." The farmer replied, "In Vermont, he's his own toad." And so the soul is its own. By a metaphysical circumstance which removes any ambiguity, authentic independence imposes responsibility for actions. This is the reasoning behind the concept of the formed conscience. The behaviorist would find that polemical. The same liberal behaviorist who would label "My country right or wrong" a paramount chauvinism, finds it's acceptable to say without reservation, "My conscience right or wrong." But to say such a thing, and leave it at that, makes senseless the absolute obligation to act according to conscience even when it is erroneous. Having rejected responsibility to universal ethical norms, the behaviorist insists that there is no Hell for those who "follow their own consciences." The truth about objective acts denies this. Moral freedom depends on my owning a conscience; it is vanquished the moment the conscience owns me.

The larger picture, without which there is no moral freedom, was indicated by St. Thomas Aquinas when he pointed out how an erroneous conscience, even when conscientiously obeyed, is nevertheless contrary to the good. If we will an act inimical to what is good, we do not make that act moral, but we do make ourselves immoral. God's gift of free will in the moral order can lead to the denial of God's greater gift of eternal life as the End of the temporal order. The heavenly economy is a "laissez-faire" economy, but it is an economy nonetheless; and that means among other things that, as we are worth "more than many sparrows," (*Luke 12:7*) we also are freer than sparrows to bankrupt ourselves. A conscience may be followed freely all the way to Hell.

This sweeping freedom discloses another dimension of God's perfection. Although he is All in All, and that is Self-Possession itself, he disdains to possess us without allowing us to possess him. Our freedom to give God permission disrupts the fatalistic pattern of false religion and the superstition of chance, and displays to the soul a reality known as Providence. God does provide for our needs, and above all else he provides himself: "Behold I am with you always, even to the end of the world." (*Matt. 28:20*) This is the way it must be, even in the context of moral freedom, because he is the End of the end, the purpose of living.

Purgatory is part of the providential arrangement. Having considered Hell, we should be able to appreciate how they are so utterly different. Purgatory is not Hell, nor is it hellish, nor is it a miniature duplication of damnation for those whose rejection of God is not so complete. God cannot be rejected partially, because he cannot leave anyone half satisfied. If a person chooses to abide with him, he abides totally, even when prayers are distracted and awareness of his presence is dimmed by an insufficient love. Purgatory is the state provided by Providence himself in which all who willed to be part of the heavenly design are shown how to do it better. Frederick Faber said it is silly to be angry at the suggestion of going to Purgatory: "Most likely it is great false flattery, and that you will never be good enough to be there at all. Why, do you not recognize your own good fortune when you are told of it. And none but the humble go there."

Talk of the fires of Purgatory then is right speech so

long as it means, as St. Francis de Sales understood it, a good fire that warms a heart which is not yet warm enough. Purgatory is the incubator of disinterested love, provided for those whose love is vital but which has not outgrown its embryonic form on earth. The Second Vatican Council (*Lumen Gentium*, N. 49) instructed: "While some of the disciples of Christ are pilgrims on earth, others who have passed from this life are being purified . . ." And this purification of the capacity for love is the channel to eternal salvation; Saint John of the Cross said that we will be asked at death only how much we loved.

Meanwhile, there is the counsel of Saint Ambrose of Milan concerning those souls now in purification, whose state and absence from those on earth can seem all too ambiguous: "We have loved them during life; let us not abandon them until we have conducted them by our prayers into the house of the Lord." What is at work here is the divine economy, but in the primitive sense of economy as having to do with a household; Purgatory is a blessed domesticity giving a tone of familiarity to the alienation of Earth and the majesty of Heaven. In compliment, Josemaria Escriva writes: "The holy souls in purgatory. Out of charity, out of justice, and out of an excusable selfishness (they have such power with God!), remember them often in your sacrifices and in your prayers. Whenever you speak of them, may you be able to say, 'My good friends, the souls in purgatory.' "

The suffering of the holy souls is a permissive access, rather of the kind Jesus enjoined: "*Suffer* the little children to come to me, for of such in the Kingdom of Heaven." (*Matt. 19:14*) In the Jacobean translation of the Greek *athete*, the benevolence of the unintentional pun on "suffer" points to how access has its dangers;

allowance to approach something also allows the possibility of hurt, and that which is being allowed the souls in Purgatory is the chance at last to adjust to an infinite brightness. If there is pain to it, the sensation is not different from that of a mother in labor, a runner panting the last stretch, a diamond cutter sweating out the final hairsbreadth between a split diamond and diamond dust. Only God knows that in this blessed state there is no possibility of any miscarriage, of yielding before the goal, or of being smashed to bits; flesh cannot revert to dust forever, so long as flesh loves enough to confess that it is dust and shall return to dust for a while. Flesh, once humbled, cannot be surprised at surpassing the diamond which is dirt under pressure, for humility is the virtue of double vision which perceives its own brilliance as great as the minutiae of its littleness. St. John of the Cross, and later St. Theresa of Lisieux, with their Carmelite spirituality longed to enter the night of shadows so as to eclipse self-preoccupation with a luminous suffering for the failings of the whole human race. Saint Catherine of Genoa called the joy of Purgatory greater than any joy on earth and less only than that of Heaven itself. But so long as we remain morally free, the potential for purgation remains tentative. We still can abort here, we can give up the race in time, we can smash the diamond so long as we hold the tools in hands of flesh. We are that free. St. Augustine said: "He who made you without your help will not save you without your cooperation."

Hell, not Purgatory, is the punishment which follows the deliberate rejection of such cooperation. There cannot be many lines so sad as these, typical of the remnant religious conscience of our own secular culture, groaned in the *Divine Comedy* by Francesca da Rimini, circling with her lover in the infernal winds:

O animal grazioso e benigno . . .
Se fosse amico il Re dell'universo
Noi pregheremmo lui per la tua pace.

O kind and gracious spirit . . .
If the King of the Universe were a friend,
We would pray to him for your peace.

There are no indicatives in the language of the damned.
Hope and certitude of divine friendship are mangled
by a battered cynicism, and come out a mocking dream,
the only mood of which is the sorrowful subjunctive of
"if" and "were."

This does not come, though, until the indications of
God are decisively rejected by human choice. God
fought to the very bounds of freedom to save his rebellious children. "He descended into Hell" between his
crucifixion and resurrection, unremarked by those who
regretted his lack of concern. Since there is no time
there, it may be that the "harrowing of Hell" was not a
day but eternity less a day.

What a dead religion it must be that does not consider
this. Alexander Pope writes in his *Moral Essays*, of one
"Who never mentions Hell to ears polite." But the descent of Jesus Christ into the very heartlessness which
buried him was an infinite politeness beyond all human
convention. With an artlessness which chills the philosopher's craft, silent Christ the High Priest crosses a divide corrupt beyond description, as though calling
across an unexplored Apheious where lie the sacred
groves of ruined Hera and Poseidon, and every other
cultic decay of unfulfilled longings.

The mind can speculate about this because Christ did
not end his "eternity save a day" in Hell when he rose

from the dead. Whenever the archaism of cynicism tries to suffocate the full breath of grace, he harrows: he harrows every family dinner table to compare what it is doing to the Heavenly Banquet, harrows every bedroom to compare it to Eden, and harrows every lecture hall to compare its declamations to the Sermon on the Mount. The passion is deeper in those encounters than the human imagination can know in its most anguished moments of love. God is not cruel to people; but the human chronicle is a thesaurus of the complex ways in which men and women have been cruel to God. By various means, celebrated and anonymous, they relentlessly humiliate his perfect love when all he ever did was to humble their very lack of it. Bigness humiliates while greatness humbles. This could, and historically probably would, remain in the loftier vaults of platitudinous information were we not given means to apply it in vital experience. It becomes the remedy against Hell when it gets put into practice through the three theological virtues of faith, hope and love.

The manualists in the moral tradition list these as three spiritual strengths which come as divine gifts. That is to say, one does not "make them happen" or garner them on one's own. It has been faddish to castigate the manualists for their "cut and dried" approach to the moral life. This is very strange at a time when manuals abound for everything else. You could hardly expect to repair a dynamo by getting an impression of it, and then tinkering with it according to intuition; a generally benign regard for energy would be helpful, but an acquaintance with the laws of thermodynamics would be more useful. Manualists wrote, and still write, against subjectivism in the order of spiritual laws, and it is still helpful to turn to them; they cut up the life of the virtues no more than the Apostle who listed the spiritual virtues and added the priority of love. If they seem dry, that can only be the fault of the reader, for it has been the experience of more than a few that the human's response to moral advice reflects the humility with which the conscience is willing to receive it. Anyway, the thing to remember is that the individual who seeks to gain Heaven and avoid Hell must be receptive, through the human practice of purity and humility and devotion, to the gifts of faith and hope and love.

Faith is needed for belief in Hell simply because the truth about Hell is that it exists as a lie. A house of mirrors exists, with all of the distortions inside it, and so it is with Hell except that Hell is invisible. The faith which is needed to see it denies credulity; the essence of faith is assent to truth activated by trust. And trust is the element which the credulous lack. The superstitious personality is a distrustful one; it exaggerates the properties of black cats and odd numbers because it does not fully assent to God's control over them; it goes so far as to attempt a manipulation of the divine order by conjuring all sorts of conundrums, passwords and, sometimes, even statistics to separate cause from effect. Once that split is allowed, then anything is allowed; and the contemporary theorist would turn terrorism into liberation, violation of human rights into pacification, infanticide into termination, all with the condescension of a Merlin holding the philosopher's stone.

Supersition is only theory, but modern man has so lapsed into credulity on occasion that he has equated speculation with fact, formula with product. Superstition is especially dangerous in executive hands. No serious harm comes from believing that babies grow under cabbage leaves; but much harm is done by saying a baby and a cabbage are the same. The latter contention is based on the magical assumption that life receives its dignity from its viability. Once this is allowed, anyone costumed with authority and equipped with a few statistics up his sleeve can intone the appropriate editorial from the *Washington Post* and turn a mother into a breeder and a nursery into a farm.

The post-modern thinker sometimes is in the position of the attendant standing behind the curtain who has learned some of the tricks. Being patient, he maintains a confidence in the "right relationship" between cause and effect, and applies this "mature" faith to the truths of causality which the modernist disguised. Meanwhile, the modernist distortion must answer, painfully, to the unhealthy cohabitation of technology and sentimentalism which has concealed the realities of Hell and Heaven, and thus has prevented the educated class from being a wise class. One result has been the lassitude of modern theology. The age of "liberal" theology has not been one of blood and steel; sentiment has made its nest in doctrinal disputations where creeds have been admitted only as dispositions. The problem is not so much that religion has become fashionable as that it has become natural; but religion is in fact unnatural unless it is supernatural. Supernatural dogma, with its claims on faith, is an unwanted intrusion into the parlor of modern credulity. Nevertheless, from the Catholic point of view, which embraces Heaven and Hell besides Earth, a religious concept of the universe which is based only on an impression of natural appearance is as eccentric as the teachings of the Flat Earth Society.

Contemporary experience needs to encounter dogma

afresh if it is to be rescued from its superstitious world-view. There is a vast difference, for instance, between the Catholic reverence for creation and the secularist's reverence for nature. If nature has not been created, it is unnatural; this is exactly the impression which the naturalist sometimes gives when elegizing its fragility. The misperception can literally push us into another stone age. A solid faith builds shrines of stone; a vicarious faith, that is, one uninformed by the intellect, simply declares the stone a shrine. Informed faith is obliged to move the salutary contemplation of nature beyond geology to theology. Otherwise the religious sensations one feels, say, when gazing at the Grand Canyon, may only confuse redemption with erosion. This does not mean you have to conclude there must be a God because there is a painted canyon; it does mean that as long as you are standing on solid ground you have no ground for denying that there might be a Heaven and a Hell.

The contemporary tendency has been to make religion the one preserve free of systematic thought, instead of letting it flourish as the intellect's primary domain. Theology properly is the queen of the sciences, and not the vassal of ignorance. Surely if some science can place a man on the moon, some other science should at least attempt a reasonable account of who put man on the earth. No modern would believe that man was pulled to the moon by the power of moon-ness, and one would believe even less that a piece of moon rock had enchanted him to itself. So the modern thinker should be just as unwilling to believe that we were placed on earth by Spinoza's "Substance" or the atheist's "Chance" as he should deny that a Melanesian tabu had done it. But he, or at least he in the current form of Western liberalism, frequently chooses the unbelievable nonetheless. This is probably why Cardinal Lustiger of Paris has said: "You are confusing a modern man with an American liberal. An American liberal isn't necessarily a modern man. The essential role of people who think is being able to reflect, and, precisely, not to give in to whatever waves are rising." The American liberal so often denies the realities of experience that he would rather re-write history than explore its cause.

The remedy indicated here is not so much a religious revival; it is more one of a religious "occural," for much of what has passed as religion even among the religious has been less than that. Authentic doctrine has to inform the modern conscience so that it might avoid the pitfalls of aimlessness, scattered attention and aroused concupiscience which are marks of incomplete faith. If the unaided intellect lacks trust in the divine hierarchy of being, it may not create paradise on earth but it will most likely build a Hades there. The same mental capacity which invented the electric light bulb in the Nineteenth Century proceeded to make lampshades of human skin in the Twentieth Century; a sobering contemplation of this must either produce a sense of abject futility, or a new regard for a higher reference which informs the intellect.

When that contemplation grows in the virtue of faith, the new age, which is post-modern, may become the realization of what was noblest in the modern longing. Man Come of Age will either become senile, or wise enough to understand that he is Man Come Back to His Senses. If wise, and this is not a fatuous utopianism, the new age may become a golden age of Catholicism as it cultivates the splendid and horrid lessons of the Twentieth Century in a universal empathy and unitive discourse unmatched since the Latin world of the high Middle Ages.

That at least is the better of the two prospects. The worse, senility of the human spirit, would cast every new invention and understanding into the tempest of venal survival, in which the egocentric criterion for truth is the sole standard of judgement. Then the materialist's banal paradise where "I am myself" would be recognized for what it is, a Hell in which "I am by myself."

Hope, the second of the theological, or infused, virtues, is a sister to faith and an antidote to Hell in that it adorns fidelity with an irresistable attractiveness, which is as lovely as the despair of the souls in Hell is ugly. There is something to be learned from the Italian word *brutto* which means both ugly and brutal; it is very civilized to be physically hurt by ugliness, for that indicates a certain moral grandeur which links aesthetics with justice. Consequently, suffering is an inevitable part of alienation from God. The suffering in Hell is not the vengeance of a cruel God but the deliberate rejection of true beauty. Unjust, or demented, passion, which leads from God and to Hell, may create fascinating things, but the deepest aestheticism will sense something repulsive in their attractiveness: a blood-red temple on a fierce pagan hill, the Golden House of a bloated Nero, and hexameters sung to demagogic destinies are remnants of true proportion and for that reason are uglier than unadorned clumsiness. For the leftover language and the entablature of sturdy inspiration are twisted into the ultimate offense against the justice of proportion; they are turned into a false beauty, which is nothing other than the most painful of charades and a true ugliness.

Calculated assymetry in the moral order, which is sin,

should affect hopefulness like nails do the flesh, as when
a carpenter calculated himself to be perfect Symmetry.
If we do not want to bear the moral responsibility of
authentic hope, we can try to take refuge in idealism,
that unreality which substitutes optimism for hopefulness and denies the justice of pain. The idealist, who
with his abstract contempt for the obvious is an indefatigable Manichean, does not understand that we are
body and soul together, and that if beauty charms the
passions, so should its denial by moral disproportion
wound them. He certainly does not understand the implications of this for the final reckoning of the moral
order. To his way of thinking, the fact of physical suffering in Hell as punishment for moral offense is out
of place. But if a headache gives me pain, and a hear-
tache gives me pain, so too must a soulache give me
pain; and this is the situation which obtains when the
conscience confronts the moral divorce from celestial
beauty. The ultimate suffering of the damned is moral,
and hurts no less physically for that. The pains of Hell
are absolutely not out of place, and are painful precisely
for being in place. When a bone is out of joint it gives
pain, but the pain is not out of joint; it is the one factor
in order. Much more is this the case when the ego is out
of joint. There is reason for hope by the very ability to
know that this is so.

The attraction of hope stimulates receptivity to faith,
of which it is a consequence. Then it plants in the soul
a different suffering of its own, the exquisite delight of
anguished anticipation, not the torment of the hopeless
but the torment of the bridegroom and bride waiting
for each other. When the perfect Symmetry wanted to
describe it for our feeble sense, he generously used this
deliberate image, blessing all who attend the unpredictable advent of the Master to the wedding.

As a passion and sentiment in the natural order, hope is limitlessly extended in the supernatural order as an affection for love. Its strength against Hell lies in its sanctifying power. As an affirmation of Saint Paul's triumphant apostrophe: "If God is for us, who can be against us?" (*Rom. 8:31*), hope dissuades the human spirit from lapsing into that sense of futility which is the crack in the wall of faith and which in its complete state is the complex of the damned. It provides an introduction to the vitality of God.

Even Christians, and even Christian clergymen, are tempted to speak of hope as some noble ideal which can sustain the spirit once faith breaks down. But hope is not a valiant *élan* meant to take the place of faith; unjustified hope is wishful thinking quite like unjustified faith. A university chaplain recently wrote that his job was to "provide a center for confusion to express itself," and while the evidence indicated that he was doing his job, it was not the job of a Christian chaplain. Sanctification requires an ordered growth in the life of the virtues, and there is no virtue in disorder. Disorder reigns when one refuses to admit the distinction between a sane contradiction and an insane confusion.

The first indication of a heresy is confusion in the description of Heaven and Hell. This confusion is based inevitably on an incapacity for contradiction; thus it has often been the case that disordered doctrine ran most rampant after Vatican II in religious communities which had long been distinguished by an aversion to inconsistency, expressed by a substitution of formalism for form. A crack will be more conspicuous on the face of a precise Vermeer painting than on a mottled surrealist work. Hope is the safeguard in such cases; its virtue understands the proper place of contradiction in the divine order and does not, for want of subtlety, confuse it with chaos. Without hope, the incapacity for contradiction can blur the vision until it is hard to tell the Beatific Vision from the concentric rings of Hell's boredom. Just as faith has to be more than faith in yourself to be authentic, so must hope be more than the modernist's stoic hope against hope. The Christian hope for heaven must be hope *with* Hope; that is, hope informed by trust in God.

The third virtue for detoxifying hellishness, Love, is indispensable. Faith is the prime virtue since it is the basis for the life of all the virtues, but Love is the motive and condition of that life. Of course, any reader knows how hard it is to speak of love in English; we have to render all meanings of love under the one inclusive word. But only the most arrested personality cannot distinguish between the nuance or inflection of the one love he or she has for ice cream and the other love for God, who put the soul in the man behind the soda fountain. This latter love is the most vivid sanctifier of the human condition. It motivates a love for perfection above all other loves. Very simply and probably maladroitly put, this love is an unhindered enjoyment of reality, since perfection is the evidence of truth, and love of that perfection is participation in it.

It is not attainable at once, because of our carnality. But, as Saint Bernard taught his brethren, it comes to be known in three stages after the soul moves beyond mere self-love. These are the love of God for the help he gives us, the love of God for the delight we find in him, and the love of God solely for his being God. The first, in Saint Thomas's categories, is the beginning or purgative stage of perfection, while the second is the illuminative and the third is the unitive, whereby divine love occupies the created soul so that God's "presence and his very self," sanctifying grace, is loving himself through human expression. The final stage is the heavenly end of the soul and, therefore, is the ultimate resolution of the convulsive illness, the divorce from God, the last station of which divorce is Hell.

A bracing attribute of the unitive stage is, dare we say it, complacency. It seems that we have lived so long among the jaded distortions of goodness that complacency has come to mean only something odious and degrading. And so it is if it is lassitude. In the supernatural order it also denotes sturdiness, serene repose in a possession which can be possessed totally because it can give itself totally. Holy complacency is the loving possession of the Possessor: the soul is possessed by God the way a flame is possessed by fire. Fire without flame is a kind of supernatural perfection, like the appearance to Moses of a fiery bush that did not burn. Flame without fire is a hellish idea, the deprivation of an essence, just as the soul without God is hellish. When the possibility becomes a circumstance, it ceases being hellish and is Hell, indescribable and inconceivable but alluded to nevertheless in a state of flame and ice, where the flame does not melt the ice nor the ice cool the flame. It is the punishment for those souls which, having been created by the perfect love of God, are possessed by the Shade which alone among all beings hates love perfectly.

The most forbidding aspect of perfect hate, daunting as the concept may be, is that, unlike anything else, it is not the opposite of its supposed opposite. While hate opposes love, it would be an exaggeration to say perfect hate opposes perfect love. The perfection of a thing brings it to its fulfillment and it becomes sufficient in itself, without contrast or opposition. Through perfection, then, hate and love are both capable of achieving a completion even when, according to the old analogy, hate finishes life by eliminating it, while love puts a finish on it, like a cabinetmaker polishing wood.

The dread secret, reserved for telling in Hell, betrays itself from time to time during the course of natural life: if perfect hate is not the opposite of perfect love, Hell still is home for some such opposite. Hate opens the gate to it; but unlike hate, the impalpable contradiction of perfect love is not a passion. The Apocalypse gives the feel of it in those parts of the vision in which an absence nearly drains the conscience of any will to continue. There is a glimpse of it in the pale horse whose gliding through the sky is more entrancing and ghastly than that of the other horses dark and bilious. It is there too at the opening of the Seventh Seal, in a stillness climaxing with an appearance of the pure intelligences who are handed incense and trumpets. It is there, in that momentary abnegation of sound, a pause on the edge of abandonment, that the possibility of an alternative to scent and harmony displays itself. The identity of this possibility is in the gasp before any trump, a sterile debauch, a weeping without tears, an incense sinking when it should rise, the intelligence of ignorance studying itself, the cloak of pride pacing around a vacuum and asking, "What next?"

To say the ultimate lovelessness cannot ever be is in fact an ostrich-like way to affirm it. The proposition can be denied only because we dwell in an earthly intimation of the void between life and death, which is the dehumanization called sin. As dissent from life in its venial species, and as alliance to death in its mortal variety, sin is the endless echo of Hell's silence. The state of sin corrupts the ability to be human about life after death. Its immediate consequence, neurosis, is an irreduceable awe before the possibility of a Real Absence. While sin assuredly has issue in socialized evil and contempt for the moral imperatives of political justice, it exists radically as a personal disobedience. Denial of this, like the denial of Hell, is self-defeating, for it only increases the emptiness which is the actual stuff of sin. To deny the Great Denial is nothing other than to join it.

While Jesus of Nazareth, King of the World, has said that he will come at the end of time to end time, casting Satan and all falseness into the burning lake (*Rev. 20:7*), he also has said how simple it is to avoid the flame and embrace the light. For while there are dreadful silences, there are the trumpets when the seals and secrets of the ages are broken, and much singing of a sort hard to audit with our present atonality. We do not know the music now, it is true. But we do know the words. And they are all we need to know, for to say them is to leave Hell a lifetime and an eternity behind. Man of the seven virtues and seven sins needs to conjoin his intellect and will, and then enter a confessional to say seven words of contrition to the priest who shares the happy and virulent struggle: "Bless me, Father, for I have sinned."

Guide me, O thou great Redeemer, Pilgrim through
    this barren land;
I am weak, but thou art mighty, Hold me with thy
    powerful hand.
Bread of Heaven, Bread of Heaven, Feed me till I
    need no more.

Open now the crystal fountain, Whence the healing
  waters flow;
Let the fire and cloudy pillar, Lead me all my journey
  through.
Mighty Savior, Mighty Savior, Ever be my strength
  and shield.

When I tread the verge of Jordan, Bid my anxious
  fears subside;
Death of death, and Hell's destruction, Land me safe
  on Canaan's side.
Songs of praises, Songs of praises, I shall ever give to
  thee.

William Williams, 1745

FOUR

SOLID HEAVEN

And in the Spirit he carried me away to a great, high mountain, and showed me the holy city Jerusalem coming down out of heaven from God, having the glory of God, its radiance like a most rare jewel, like a jaspar, clear as crystal. It had a great, high wall, with twelve gates, and at the gates twelve angels, and on the gates the names of the twelve tribes of the sons of Israel were inscribed; on the east three gates, on the north three gates, on the south three gates, and on the west three gates. And the wall of the city had twelve foundations, and on them the twelve names of the twelve apostles of the Lamb. And he who talked to me had a measuring rod of gold to measure the city and its gates and walls. The city lies foursquare, its length the same as its breadth; and he measured the city with his rod, twelve thousand stadia (about fifteen hundred miles); its length and breadth and height are equal. He also measured its wall, a hundred and forty-four cubits by a man's measure, that is, an angel's. The wall was built of jaspar, while the city was pure gold, clear as glass. The foundations of the wall

of the city were adorned with every jewel; the first
was jaspar, the second sapphire, the third agate, the
fourth emerald, the fifth onyx, the sixth carnelian,
the seventh chrysolite, the eighth beryl, the ninth to-
paz, the tenth chrysoprase, the eleventh jacinth, the
twelfth amethyst. And the twelve gates were twelve
pearls, each of the gates made of a single pearl, and
the street of the city was pure gold, transparent as
glass. And I saw no temple in the city, for its temple
is the Lord God the Almighty and the Lamb. And the
city has no need of sun or moon to shine upon it, for
the glory of the God is its light, and its lamp is the
Lamb. By its light shall the nations walk; and the kings
of the earth shall bring their glory into it, and its gates
shall never be shut by day—and there shall be no
night there; they shall bring into it the glory and the
honor of the nations. But nothing unclean shall enter
it, nor any one who practices abomination or false-
hood, but only those who are written in the Lamb's
book of life. (*Rev. 21:10-27*)

Most men and women who think seriously enough to
take Heaven seriously, prefer life on earth. Heaven
seems hazy and we do not want to be in the shade. Given
the choice, the flesh-and-blood naturalist would rather
be gouty than ghostly. Given the choice, that is, as a
naturalist might define it. But by putting the choice that
way, the naturalist becomes something like the prohi-
bitionist who said he would sooner commit adultery than
drink sherry. We have far more autonomy in supernatural choices than in natural ones. No Joshua ever
told the trembling tribes to choose between air on earth
and asphyxia in Heaven. Joshua did say "Choose this
day whom you will serve." On the way to the Golden
City, the New Joshua, who is Christ, pleaded with the
whole nation to make a choice and follow him.

He anticipated, though, that Israel, which stood for
the human race, would hesitate to choose a supernatural
goal for its natural sojourn. When he appeared from

the dead he kept saying, "Shalom." But still the people
were fearful for the incontestable reason that they knew
he had died. So he replied, "Why are you troubled? And
why do thoughts arise in your hearts? Behold my hands
and feet, that it is I myself; handle me and see; for a
serpent does not have flesh and bones as you see I have."
(*Luke 24:38-40*) The apostles' reaction was the inevitable
price we pay for having set capricious limits on the op-
erations of truth. They thought it was too good to be
true. Only the modern optimist thinks that something
might be too bad to be true; and no one ever seems to
have thought something might be too bad to be false.
But the odd concept of a thing too good to be true has
been so widely accepted that it has become not a paradox
but a truism. The apostles fell for it. Their instincts sent
them back fishing, the stunned sort of thing people do
in shock; it was, if you will, the first half of a doubletake,
the coiling up before the recoil. That which the apostles
thought was too abstract to be real had suddenly become
too solid for them to confront.

If this is shock, it is metaphysical shock; and, like any
other kind of trauma, it is caused by an assault on a
routine expectation. The naturalist may profess to be
shocked by the idea of ghosts, and he would certainly
be shocked to see a ghost if such things existed; but
more irretrievably would he be shocked to encounter
someone who *should* be a ghost and yet refuses. In his
arbitrarily defined materialism, the naturalist compro-
mises himself by setting up a moral standard for determining existence. Just as he assumes in his engaging
optimism that Hell is an absurdity, too bad to be true,
so he rebounds into a corresponding pessimism which
decides Heaven must be a fantasy, too good to be true.
This bobbing back and forth is the opposite of temper-

amental balance; it is a neurosis. And, unlike Hell and Heaven, this neurosis is completely unfounded; that actually is what makes it neurotic. There are no physical proofs for it, no chemical evidence or mathematical probability. All the naturalist can present as evidence for what he thinks does not exist is a moral argument, and moral arguments are heresies according to his own naturalism which claims never to say "ought" or "ought not" but "is" and "is not."

The supernaturalist is more scientific; he does not have to reject any element of nature to illustrate his point. The risen Christ's metaphysics were a cooperative function of natural physics. He obliged the apostles by showing them his ability to eat naturally. While most of moralizing Jerusalem hid behind closed shutters away from the evidence, an empirical exercise in heavenliness was conducted in that one meeting room of the apostolic college. In keeping with everything else Jesus had taught about Heaven, it involved eating.

If he was not a ghost, what manner of life was he? In the Easter sunset on the Emmaus road, he looked like an ordinary man, and was actually mistaken for a pedestrian, yet he was not recognizable to his two friends. If anonymity cloaked him, no monstrous distortion did; he was perfectly unremarkable in appearance. Only his speech was of interest. In the reversal of that dusk, at dawn of the same day, Mary Magdalene had distractedly confused him with the gardener; again it was his speech which compelled. He refused to be touched by her; but then, again, the apostles recognized him at once and he challenged Thomas to touch him. It is not known for a fact whether Thomas did accept the challenge, but the Rabbi clearly was touchable. And it was equally palpable that he would not be manipulated.

You can summarize the evidence. This figure once dead and now apparently alive looks commonplace and sounds extraordinary; he is graciously accommodating and equally refuses to be accommodated; he is personal and attentive, and he is practically ubiquitous, appearing in rapid succession in places far apart; his body passes through closed doors and is still capable of eating solid food. It can best be said in a reserved way that he is visible and, if not what would be called a typical person, an active personality.

At the beginning of this book we considered the difference between invisible objects which cannot be seen anywhere, and unseen objects which are just out of view. Analyzed the other way, a visible figure can be seen by anyone while a seeable figure is one that has come out of concealment. It is the difference between what can be seen and what may be seen, and on this hangs the distinction between what can be and what may be. To say that things visible and invisible are nothing other than things seen and unseen gives the impression that this is a game of hide-and-seek. At worst, it implies that there is no invisible reality. The human personality would have to contradict itself to believe that, since the personality is the most immediate invisibility of our human being.

This personality is the perceptible and equally undepictable "subject of attribution," to use a phrase of St. Thomas, capable of intelligence and desire, of awareness and projection. It is an individuation which precedes liberty; and even existence is a contingent attribute of it. If it cannot be painted or photographed, it is nonetheless vivid in the smile and frown of the human face over against the grin and snarl of the beast's jowls. You could say that man and beast have heads but only man has a face. Anthropologists in search of the first human possibly spend too much time measuring skulls and too little time measuring laughs. A laugh is not a refined shriek, it is something wholly new; and so man is not an improvement of an earlier biped, but an original gift to creation with the first flurry of a smile, not an ever-increasing echo and higher intelligence, but an inspiration and a completely new knowledge. If there is a "missing link" it is frozen in the world's first pout and bottled with the world's first wink. It is whatever caused the antediluvian clay to first flare nostrils breathing reason and will, and is of that first instant when instinct became insight, habit a choice, and migration a new thing called a vacation. The outcome is named the image of God.

This divine image, or personality, had a celestial play on the road to Emmaus. First the resurrected Lord demanded of the reason, "Why are you sad?" and then at table he elicited an affirmation of the will as he broke the bread, connecting in one sequence the logic of Melchizedek and Moses and himself. In the lush Easter garden he required of the Magadelene's intellect, "Why are you weeping?" and then under the enamelled sky he animated her individuality by uttering her name. Saint Gregory the Great mimed for Christ: "Recognize him, by whom you are recognized. Not generally as the others, but particularly, do I know you." Definiteness, said John Henry Newman, is the secret to speaking heart to heart; that is, we do have personalities and to be random, to be a shotgun instead of a rifle, is always to miss the human essence. Queen Victoria complained that Gladstone addressed her as though she were a public meeting; Disraeli captivated her affection by lyricising as though she were the only creature in the world. Such

was graciousness on Disraeli's part; with Jesus it is grace.
To human perception, beauty may in some degree be
in the eye of the beholder; with the King of Beauty, it
is the eye of the Beholder who "beheld all things and
saw that they were very good." (*Gen. 1:31*) Delight in
restored creation, then, is the characteristic of divine
definiteness; and its marvellousness is clarion in the distinctiveness of each personality, which the Scholastics
called the incommunicable "I," not two of which are
identical among the flashing billions ever made.

An impatience with vaguery, then, is a discernable
characteristic of the divine image. By way of corollary,
it is a sign that Heaven is definite and, so to speak,
solid—solid, that is, as the risen body of Christ, capable
of gnawing bones and vanishing into clouds in one and
the same universe. The dislike for half-states is suggested materially in our own inherited condition; were
not God's image implanted in each of us, we should have
a spontaneous affinity for ghosts, half truths, unfinished
paintings, picture frames hung lopsidedly on the wall,
miscarriages of infants and miscarriages of justice, treble
clefs without bass clefs, unresolved card games and
clashing colors. If obsession with these frustrations is a
symptom of retentiveness, it is because the interior sense
of proportion retains a recollection of a seventh day
after the sixth day of creation, a wholeness which is the
fabric of beauty, and a holiness which is the substance
of truth. More than memory, the soul retains a promise
of some new kingdom where the law of harmony will
have perfect sway and where the broken-toothed lions
and half-sheared lambs will be true lions and true lambs
side by side in vernal peace. The recollection of the old
garden is the intimation of the New Jerusalem. Heaven
will more than irrigate and reclaim Eden. It will make

it a habitable city with no possibility of ruin. People fit into gardens; they are made fit for cities.

A due sense of moral proportion outfits us for the Heavenly City and, as we have observed, this is expressed concretely in the concept of completeness. Only because there is a real Heaven do we have the notion of a finishing touch. When someone interjects, "Wait a minute. Let me fix it. There!" we are listening to an ever so modest reverberation of the Carpenter's *Consummatum est* called from crossed wood. And if that is memory, then the future hope believes that when death cracks our frame and threatens our spirit, we will hear the same voice ten thousand times louder: "Wait a minute. Let me fix it. There!" It will sound, as it did once before, like an earthquake.

Anything less than the whole cannot be wholly true; and anything less than solid cannot be bliss. The whole truth of angels becomes deceitful when confused with human nature; the glory of man is to be found to some extent in his distinction from angelic glory: "For thou hast made him a little lower than the angels, and hast crowned him with glory and honor." (*Psalm 8:5*) As human and not angelic, we are other than messengers of God, for we are able to be bearers of God himself, *theophoroi*. Gregory of Nyssa, in *De Instituto Christiano,* drew on the unique place of man in the hierarchy of being, possessing the intelligence which animals lack and the perception which angels lack, to account for our singular likeness to Christ. As a result of this similitude, human beings literally can take charge of creation, as not even the greatest angels are allowed, once they conform to God's intelligence and will.

To deny angels their celestial integrity is humanism; to deny humans their earthly integrity is angelism. Both open the door to bestialism which is the groggiest fantasy of all, like believing a prince can be turned into a frog by the incantations of an expert in behaviorism. Obviously there is much about human behavior which is like animal behavior, but objective conduct is not subjective destiny. Moral striving for an eternal reward, as it is peculiar to human nature, is different from the sort of behavior which is patterned to receive gratification and avoid pain; it actually involves drinking of a bitter cup and bathing in cold water and even blood (see *Matt. 20:22-23; Mark 10:38-39*). For man is neither angel nor beast but man, and the failure to get this balance straight is what constitutes the secular humanist's lack of humanity; but as such, man's especial glory and honor gratify him only when he has first gratified God. Man must worship to be human. Garrigou-Lagrange said, "By vision the soul possesses God, and by love it rejoices in him, and rests in him; it prefers him to itself, as one prefers the infinite to a poor finite good." This heavenly vision does not deprive man of his world even as it contradicts that world's temporal inadequacies; it makes him Master of the world, fulfilling the primeval investiture of Adam with authority to name all living things.

Consequently, half of any truth has to give only half the picture, like the interference on a television set, and dismally like the cobweb state of Sheol, the shadowy land of the half living with which the later Hebraic cosmology half-heartedly consoled itself; there the dead had not worth for they would not worship God (*Isa. 38:18*) and the remembrance of Adam's potent mantel mocked their desiccation. A few hundred years before the birth of Christ the vision sharpened; the prophet Daniel wrote, "Many of those that sleep in the dust of the earth shall awake: some unto life everlasting." (*Dan. 12:2*)

Even this more animated apocalyptic material is less like
peering into a diamond sky and more like airing a long
shut cedar chest. Nor had all the strugglers been the
chosen Jews. The problematic description of life after
death seems to have been nearly universal. It would be
a vacant lethargy that is not appalled by the heroic sadness which distills the pagan sixth book of the *Aeneid* as
Aeneas describes the departure of his mother Venus:
"Thrice I tried to throw my arms around her neck, and
thrice grasped in vain. The image fled the hands like
light winds and very like a fleeting dream."

But this twilight melancholia of a void after life is not
the disposition of Christianity as it awaits the afterlife;
that is, the Heaven promised by Christ would not be
Heaven were it a state after a life, for Heaven comes
after a death. It proposes life in more abundant intensity
precisely for that. Heaven is attained after being raised
from the dead, and that to which the dead are raised
in nothing less than life fulfilled: "So you have sorrow
now, but I will see you again and your hearts will rejoice,
and no one will take your joy from you." (*John 16:22*)
The Rabbi abolished forever any excuse for wistful contemplation of a demi-career in a hollow fog. Every aversion to such a dank and stale shallowness is a whisper
saying we have been created to inherit more than a part
of the whole.

The part remains an option. The human annals show
how many thinkers have tantalized themselves with half-
life in their various indulgences of reason without self-
awareness. The tendency moved to full rational steam
after the Renaissance; Catholic reason was replaced with
an individualistic veneration for the technique of reason,
that is, the concern for freedom of conscience purely
for conscience's sake. But, without the reference of tran-

scendent truth, this constrained the rational dialectic
with dire results. A charismatic intuition yielded to material syncretism and a resulting confusion about the
cause of dignity and hope. In the social order, as Arnold
Toynbee observed, Catholic anthropology found itself
rejected in favor of an idealized tribalism in the post-
Reformation disintegration. The modern Teutonism of
the Nazis was its Dionysian apogee, but even the schematic optimism of good men breathed it in; hence, for
example, there was the racism of Teilhard de Chardin
which embarrasses his students even as it wafts like a
wail behind his dithyrambs to universal goodness.

In the secular development of the Nineteenth Century, an exagerrated idealism had transformed rationalism into a virtual worship of the rare Genius. Now the
Genius was ill-defined, but nevertheless functioned in
place of the Holy Spirit as the authentication of wisdom,
consequently promoting expression over inspiration.
The result was desultory; the illegitimate optimism proposed hope without an adequate cause, certainly not a
divine cause, and so began the descent to a sinister pessimism. Schopenhauer's dark boast, "I think with my
stomach," was basically as indigestible as the sunny rationalist's belief in the possibility of man eating with his
mind, as though there really were such a thing as food
for thought, and that if we chewed enough equations
we would be properly nourished.

The bright neo-classical atria of the *philosophes* had
slipped almost imperceptibly into the neo-gothic pavill-
lions of romance, and what had been doric and lucid
gently sank into an agreeable absentmindedness replete
with amber odes to ruined abbeys, over-varnished land-
scapes, slow violins and faint French horns. It was as if
the imagination could be aided by blurring the objects

of speculation and setting them off at a distance. Every age has wanted to be farsighted, but this was the first to think it involved an eye condition; each generation has tried to look through a crystal ball but the Romantics were the first to think they could do it from inside the ball.

With the advent of psychological materialism, the ineffable Genius was democratized by the very proletarianism it had championed. It soon became the claim of everyone who agreed that the Genius is whatever makes you feel good. Instead of the *salonistes* banding together to audit Chopin, we have come to the nuclear family unit in which each member is plugged separately into televisions, home computers and stereo sets. Romantic languor, having yielded to the baleful melancholy of blues music generations ago, has now entered its more nihilistic resolution in hard rock; hard indeed it is, not because it is difficult but because it is obdurate. When Reason yields to Genius and Genius yields to Self Expression, a species of moral atrophy sets in. The Encyclopaedist's twinkly eye freezes, the Romanticist's dreamy eye freezes, the Existentialist's rheumy eye freezes; and at the end of the corridor is a glazed stare, sight without vision, and a remnant intellect which registers all intuition as an optical illusion. Such is the curse of Narcissus, the patron of all who become insensible to the vital source of hope beyond the limited assumptions and projections of the self. Not by mere happenstance does the name Narcissus and the word narcotic have the same root, *narké*, which means numbness. The illusion of a reality is only a self-projection, as Narcissus found to be the tragic case when he spurned the voice of Echo for his own reflection in the water. It numbs the capacity for truly human acts, as happens when food, sex, wealth and work are used as narcotics for the ego. And that, in turn, freezes our vision of eternal life as the cause and substance of hope.

Optimism's tortured abuse, as it has in one way or another affected all materialist philosophy, is absolutely absent from the mystical descriptions of Heaven. The saints are too occupied with visions to waste time on illusions, and so Paul Claudel said that everything must be either allusion or illusion. Heaven is that to which all solidity alludes. Celestial poetry is golden verse; the landscape of it is crystal and its music is definite, no muffled drums or saxophones. The holy mystics clean up the visage of optimism somewhat the way art restorers can clean the face of a Sienese madonna and who, by so doing, may upset the occasional aesthete who had come to admire the grime.

The Romanticist who admires patina and the nihilist who likes dirt can be equally depressing. Both clash against the mystical writers who can be chilling or befuddling but who cannot objectively be said to depress. This in turn is another intimation of the heavenly design. Depression is a phenomenon only because humans, having been created in the divine image, can be *im*-pressed. A deflated balloon is a balloon nonetheless; to say there is a valley is one way of saying there are hills; we are Lent only because we are Carnival. When the Voice says, "I will see you again, and your heart shall rejoice, and your joy no man will take from you" (*John 16:22*), he means that we are capable of joy in the first place. Religious people sometimes convey this as clumsily as the skeptics. It must have been after having been told that Heaven is where you are not allowed to drink or dance that the pundit coined the phrase "Heaven for climate, Hell for society." But to the contrary, in anticipation of the social joys of Heaven, Christ told his disciples, "You know not what manner of spirit you are. For the Son of Man is come not to destroy men's lives but to save them." (*Luke 9:55-56*)

To save lives. An artist saved Winston Churchill's repose during his "wilderness years" when she found him frustrated in the garden, painting timid strokes on a new canvass; she showed him how to make a few bold strokes and later, with rooms full of paintings behind him, he announced that he intended to spend the first ten thousand years in Heaven painting pictures in the brightest colors. Jesus tried to rescue the rich young man with bold strokes, telling him to give away nothing less than his whole heart, and he tried it too with the stingy men in the story of the widow's coins (*Matt. 19:16-22; Luke 18:18-23; Mark 12:41-44; Luke 21:1-4*). Of such bold strokes, he said, is the kingdom of Heaven. And of such, then, is our spirit. The kingdom of Heaven can only be taken by a force which does violence to pettiness and meanness and the discounting of glory, human and divine. This is the one battle which gives peace, and the one violence which is serene: "From the days of John the Baptist until now the kingdom of Heaven has suffered violence, and men of violence take it by force." (*Matt. 11:12*) Love abundant can risk being plundered, and the Kingdom of Divine Love invites the plunderer in with songs of welcome. The good thief of Good Friday became good when he stole Paradise.

The reference to timid paint strokes suggests two other fallacies about Heaven: that it is boring and that it is an escapist fantasy. To maintain the first is like a drowning man who refuses to be pulled to shore for fear he will have nothing interesting to do on the beach. As to the insistence that the notion of Heaven is a distraction from the difficulties of life on earth, history usurps theory. The most acute sense of social justice has consistently been prompted by the moral equilibrium which comes from the promise of Heaven and the coefficient assurance that Heaven can begin on earth: "Thy Kingdom come, thy will be done on earth as it is in Heaven." Only a non-sacramental pietism such as accompanies any decline in Eucharistic consciousness has been able to divorce this immanence of Heaven from the daily life of Christians. Rather, this is the very substance of classical Christian liturgy since it brings Heaven to the altar of earth. The singing of the prayers of the divine office is a priestly intercession along with the Eucharist, and the canticle is that which is sung in the halls of Heaven. We cannot say it is sung at the same time because there is no time in Heaven, and hence no coincidence, but we can say it is sung through the same Christ (see *Constitution on the Sacred Liturgy*, Vatican II, N. 83).

This sublime Catholic vision requires an appreciation of the divinization to which humans in creation are called, and this also means that a line has to be drawn between secularisation and secularism. While colloquially they are the same, they are fundamentally opposed in the spiritual order of creation as rationalization is opposed to reason. The Fathers of the Second Vatican Council propounded the contrast (*Gaudium et Spes*, N. 36):

> Many of our contemporaries seem to fear that if human activity is too closely bound up with religion the autonomy of men, of society and of the sciences will be thwarted. If by the autonomy of earthly realities we mean that created things and even societies have laws and values proper to themselves, which mankind must gradually discover, use and regulate, then we

are dealing with a legitimate demand which not only is put forward by men of our time but also in conformity with the will of the Creator. For by the very circumstances of their having been created, all things are endowed with their own stability, truth, goodness, proper laws and order. Man must respect these as he isolates them by the appropriate methods of the individual sciences or arts. Therefore if methodical investigation within every branch of learning is carried out in a genuinely scientific manner and in accord with moral norms, it never truly conflicts with faith, for earthly matters and the concerns of faith derive from the same God. Indeed whoever labors to penetrate the secrets of reality with a humble and steady mind, even though he is unaware of the fact, is nevertheless being led by the hand of God, who holds all things in existence, and gives them their identity . . . But if the expression, "the independence of earthly realities" is taken to mean that created things do not depend on God, and that man can use them without any reference to their Creator, anyone who acknowledges God will see how false such a meaning is. For without the Creator the creature would disappear. For their part, however, all believers of whatever religion always hear His revealing voice in the discourse of creatures. When God is forgotten, however, the creature itself grows unintelligible.

Suffice it to say, for example, that there never was a true hospital that was not a "Hotel-Dieu." Before the modern development of medical science, hospitals were indeed only places for the youngest and oldest to die. But that was at least a heavenly realism. Since the decline of the celestial vision through secularisation, the meaning of the creature has become increasingly obscure, and hospitals have become places for the youngest and oldest to be killed. Infanticide and euthanasia are forms of the secularizer's escapism. Like the real prospect of being hanged, in Dr. Johnson's estimation, the prospect of going to Heaven concentrates the mind wonderfully. It is no more an escape from life than maturity is an escape from baby clothes. Of course the personality cannot go back to innocence, but it can grow into righteousness. Saints in fact can be innocent as doves only to the extent that they are wise as serpents (*Matt. 10:16*). But the Messianic counsel tends to be lost on the critic who says in the same breath that Catholicism is anti-social and a form of social imperialism, and who then blames the inconsistency on hypocrisy. Fantasy gave us Peter Pan; Heaven gave us Joan of Arc. In fantasy Robin Hood stole money from the rich to give to the poor; in heavenly fact, Vincent de Paul stole poverty from the poor and gave it to the rich. And the rich, so blessed, treated it as an endowment.

Victims of secularization can be astonishingly naive about practical affairs, and so can the spurious pietists. But the saints never are. The secular idealists, and not the mystics, believed in the indomitable force of progressivism and thus became what Lenin called his "useful idiots." But a saint, with his eyes on Heaven, brings no useful idiocy to any tyrant. He is more of a menace. The anthropocentric materialist is easily exploited because he does not see the whole picture; he sees only the temporal portion of the world which was given to him at Creation, and that is as obtuse as looking at a painting and seeing only paint. The celestial perspective is far more organic than that. It cannot figure as "pie in the sky;" it is why we enjoy the taste of pie on earth, and bless Heaven for it. It is not the silver cup at the end of a race; it is the race. Job called it warfare (*7:1*).

The Catholic mystical vision is both luscious and calamitous. The unimaginative sensuality of Islamic paradise is alien to it, but neither is it cloaked in the cerebral silence of the Buddhist's Heaven. The Heaven of Christ has a translucency such as dignified Boticelli's sensibility. Certainly the secularizer has never approximated such depiction; his efforts to symbolize vitality have ended up regularly in the form of cramped polemicism found in some of the murals in New Deal post offices. If one has nothing to preach, one becomes preachy. These social genre paintings, like those of Rivera and Orozco and the Stalinist realists, are sympathetic in style to Goebbel's advocacy art of the Third Reich. If you go far enough left you are bound to meet those who kept moving to the right. This can only be denied if we think the world of ideas is flat, which is what happens to the victimized promoters of a dialectical international socialism or an imposed national socialism or, for that matter, a gullible consumerism. Human expression falls flat without a heavenly ideal. Art without a celestial connection will always be eclectic and unadventurous. A painting of happy factory workers done in the 1930's style totally lacks the subversive force of, say, those paradisical citizens drawn by Giovanni di Paolo in the 1430's style. And the attempt to confound this beleaguered ugliness, without transcendent allusion, will only end up contradictory, such as happened with the abstractionist experiments.

Paintings can be hidden easily enough, but we have been trapped by architects in more permanent monuments to the arrogance of secularization. The functional style of Gropius and his apprentices have cramped man into a superficiality so extensive that it gives the impression of being profound, when it is only an institutionalization of the desire to be international at the expense of becoming universal. They intended to construct something for the "common man," as though the common man were commonplace. The Christian has been aware that the common man is an uncommon animal because of his yearning for a heavenly home. Therefore his worldly habitations should not compromise the dignity of living. A slum is an intolerable offense to this proportionate reality, but so too is the brutalism of the design by which some societies try to remedy the slum. Brutality is a form of poverty, possibly the worst form, since it isolates individuals from their individuality. Loneliness is the basic poverty. It is possible to make a case for saying that the circumstances of alienation increased with Victorian sanitary housing reform and then became the assumed necessary consequence of Twentieth Century architectural orthodoxy. It propagated the idea that human destiny is to be functional but not something deeper called exalted.

Mass production produced more comfort for more people, but it failed to increase human dignity, if beauty is a sign of it. Before the Industrial Revolution there may have been too few easy chairs, but there were no ugly chairs; rooms may have been cold but they were not chilling. The hearth is nothing if it does not warm the heart. Authentic confidence in Heaven can preserve men and women from being imposed upon by theorists who claim progress is less than a pilgrimage toward a Heart at the center of the universe. For evidence of the indomitable longing for the world beyond this world, Polycarp and Savanarola on burning pyres and refugees facing gunfire across the Berlin Wall are magnificent; but so, too, is any tenant who defies his landlord by putting an electric log in a cardboard fireplace to make it feel more like home.

While the most humane and effective social institutions have been the work of people with their eyes on Heaven, the worst human catastrophes have been engineered by people with their eyes on the ground. Adjusting the scales of temporal justice without recourse to Heaven as the standard measure is as unreliable as learning to count from one to twelve by rolling a pair of dice. The lack of adequate reference helped carve the gulf between Carrie Nation smashing the whiskey bottles and Matthew Talbot smashing the addiction, and more portentously it contrasts Margaret Sanger advocating the reduction of certain racial groups with Mother Teresa reclaiming the poorest of the poor. Miss Sanger did not succeed in solving the over-population of poor countries, although she prepared the way for what is becoming the underpopulation of rich countries. Mother Teresa has not increased starvation by rescuing infants, but she has identified a new impoverishment of the spirit in the best nourished societies. In tracing the progress of social justice, the one generalization which holds valid and which may be maintained without temerity is this: a reformer who does not hope to form souls for Heaven is quite likely to become a reformer with a vendetta.

Once the consciousness dismisses the deep Heaven-consciousness of Christ and confines Messianic history to a symbolic system of moral myths, it begins to think that the Resurrection narratives are deficient in social burden. In that light the narratives do appear totally insensitive to problematic discourse and could be called immoral on those grounds. During the fifty days between the Resurrection and the Ascension, the risen Christ exhibited a cavalier disregard for many persistent matters. If he had not been, to the satisfaction of some, omnipotent and omnipresent before then, he certainly was by then, and yet he appears to have made no attempt to improve mass transit; he showed no one how to vaccinate against smallpox and gave not the slightest intimation of Robert's Rules of Order. A Leonardo or a Benjamin Franklin would have done these and more unstintingly, but our Lord left such undertakings for Mr. Ford, Mr. Jenner and Mr. Robert. Christ did not teach the method for pasteuring or macadamizing, and so today we do not drink christianized milk or ride christianized highways. For some of the more intense reformers this is a loss. They do not notice, however, that he did christianize wine.

Much of his resurrection language, when you think of it, had to do with food and on one occasion he actually did the cooking. An unlikely culinary preoccupation fills the discourses. From the bowels of a great mystery did he tell Peter, "Feed my sheep" and the fathoming of that source depends on the principle which brought him to the cross: it is useless to reform the world until the world is first *trans*formed. And it is quite as futile to speak of doing anything to my world unless it is also done to me. The cooking and eating in Easter dawnlight demonstrates how the soul transformed is a festal soul: "I will greatly rejoice in the Lord, my soul shall be joyful in my God; for he hath clothed me with the garments of salvation, he hath covered me with the robe of righteousness, as a bridegroom decketh himself with ornaments, and as a bride adorneth herself with her jewels." (*Isa. 61:10*) We shall not be at a feast in Heaven, for we shall in some way be the feast. We shall "hunger no more, nor thirst any more," (*Rev. 7:16*) and this will be so not by loss of appetite, but because we shall be in the living presence of the Source of all desire.

Consequently, when Jesus says that in Heaven there is neither marrying nor giving in marriage, he does not fairly mean that the charisms of personal union will

vanish. He reveals with the greatest chivalry how Heaven
is the marriage itself and no attempt at contact is needed
for no one in Heaven is ever out of touch. On our al-
ienated planet, the charade of this which is called free
love will gasp and pale before freed love in Heaven. But
any further attempt at explanation would be fraught
with silliness or vulgarity just now. The thing to remember is the limitation of that word "now" when we are
speaking of such things; they belong to eternity which
Boethius called "the perfect and simultaneous total possession of unending life." Souls purged of their sins are
in that "perpetual now" even as we are trying to define
it; but we also know that, with the exception of the
Blessed Virgin Mary, bodily identity will not be reunited
to the soul's identity until the general resurrection of
the dead at the culmination of history.

This must further restrict our speculation, as it did
the Apostle's. While he expected, by a wisdom vouchsafed to him alone, that there would be a series of heavenly states (*2 Cor. 12:2-4*), Saint Paul did not quite
explain whether Heaven is definitively a state of being
or a state of extra dimensions. He demurred with sa-
gacity when it came to the What as well as the Where
of it: "Eye has not seen, ear has not heard, nor has it so
much as dawned on man what God has prepared for
those who love Him." (*1 Cor. 2:9*) He meant *our* eyes,
but certainly not Christ's; for those singular eyes had
seen and heard sights and sounds which imperfect humanity cannot bear. No one with ambition for a full
humanity can consign to a corner of inattention the solemn and wondrous record which says he˙ "raised" his
eyes to Heaven (*Mark 6:41; John 17:1*).

One might hope for the ability to be constant when
the gift is given, as Saint Stephen was when he was per-

mitted by the grace of martyrdom to raise his eyes that
way. And the soul, which is intent on establishing its full
humanity, must also resolve to do all it can in discour-
aging the curious onlookers from covering their ears
when the canticle of Heaven starts to reach earth (see
Acts 7:55-57).

> That the earthly and the heavenly city penetrate each
> other is a fact accessible to faith alone; it remains a
> mystery of human history, which sin will keep in great
> disarray until the splendor of God's sons is fully re-
> vealed. Pursuing the saving purpose which is proper
> to her, the Church does not only communicate divine
> life to men but in some way casts the reflected light
> of that life over the entire earth, most of all by its
> healing and elevating impact on the dignity of the
> person, by the way in which it strengthens the seams
> of human society and imbues the everyday activity of
> men with a deeper meaning and importance. Thus
> through her individual members and her whole com-
> munity, the Church believes she can contribute greatly
> toward making the family of man and its history more
> human. (*Gaudium et Spes*, N. 40).

As for the transformation beyong reformation, which
the beatific soul enjoys, Saint Paul says that we shall not
sleep but we shall be changed: ". . . for the trumpet shall
sound, and the dead shall be raised incorruptible, and
we shall be changed." (*1 Cor. 15:51-52*) We shall be unlike what we were, but we would not be even half human
if we did not beg more: how, to be precise, shall we be
changed? Since the Apostle was human he posed the
rhetorical question: "Some man will ask, How are the
dead raised up? and with what body do they come!" (*1
Cor. 15:35*) Then he calls his unseen interlocutor foolish,
which indeed he is as are we all; but this does not satisfy
the desire for specifics, as no earthly language can. Saint
Thomas Aquinas tried his best, saying the risen body

will be incorruptible, impassible, agile, subtle and glorious. But how much change can we undergo and still be ourselves? Is there a physical trauma analogous to the social trauma of change which our society has known in this century?

Twentieth Centuryists, who speak as though this were the definitive age, would improve their perspective by recognizing that the Twentieth Century will end before the infants being born, as these lines are being written, reach legal drinking age. By then they will scarcely appreciate what it means to say that these hundred years have seen more technical changes in science and culture than the last thirty-five hundred years combined. Men and women who remembered life before the horseless carriage lived to see a man walking on the moon. As change is necessary for life, increased change should mean an increased liveliness. This has obviously happened objectively in terms of life expectancy and, more subjectively, the enjoyment of daily pleasures has increased for many by various material factors. But the peril to life has also increased. The moral significations of change parallel the ambiguities of physical change; by the same token we are morbidly aware that to grow and to have a growth are opposite things. All of our body cells are replaced every seven years; that is health. When it happens every seven months, that is cancer. When does change stop forming John Doe and begin to deform him?

Sometimes former celebrities get asked by passers-by, "Didn't you used to be so-and-so?" When the silent film star was told that she "used to be so big," she replied, "I still am big. It's the pictures that got small." But resurrection is not akin to that memory living off its fantasies; nor is it like the snake shedding its skin. The transformation worked by the resurrection guides the essential personality through the mirror so that we live as the self and not as the self's reflection, thus conquering the aleination from the self which is the consequence of sin.

Resurrection is both divinization and humanization, and in the proper ordering of creation the gift of eternal life reveals the similitude between the two. The diabolic temptation to be as gods was wrong because it seduced man from the deeper gift of being in God:

> And you he made alive, when you were dead through the trespasses and sins in which you once walked, following the course of this world, following the prince of the power of the air, the spirit that is now at work in the sons of disobedience. Among these we all once lived in the passions of our flesh, following the desires of the body and mind, and so we were by nature children of wrath, like the rest of mankind. But God, who is rich in mercy, out of the great love with which he loved us, even when we were dead through our trespasses, made us alive together with Christ (by grace you have been saved), and raised us up with him, and made us sit with him in the heavenly places in Christ Jesus, that in the coming ages he might show the immeasurable riches of his grace in kindness toward us in Christ Jesus. For by grace you have been saved through faith; and this is not your own doing, it is the gift of God—not because of works, lest any man should boast. For we are his workmanship, created in Christ Jesus for good works, which God prepared beforehand, that we should walk in them. (*Eph. 2:1-10*)

The less a person understands this recovery of personality, the less he tends to smile. This is not an aside. Saint Thomas says that to be human is to be able to smile. As we have already allowed in discussing the economy of reason and will in the discernment of personality,

humanity is "risability." This congenial idea of the school
men makes more psychological sense than any number
of pediatric surgeons and geronologists inventing cri-
teria for measuring the quality of life. If we are to draw
a limit to how much we can change while remaining
ourselves, the intolerable change will have to include the
abolition of risability. Secularization threatens to make
homo sapiens a brute by taking away his gift for delight,
and the extent to which it is succeeding is apparent in
the decline of the smile in both consumerist and collec-
tivist societies. The alteration is a mutation; humaneness
should refuse to pretend that it is progressive transformation. It is a particularly painful mutation because it
replaces the King of Heaven with a dictator called the
Super Ego; and Hell then extends its domain in a dem-
iurge called the Id. The magnificent resurrection of the
species into heavenly glory "by the power which enables
(Christ) to subject all things to himself" and its power
to engage in "heavenly conversation" (see *Phil. 3:20-21*)
are thus endangered by a devolution into constant interior conflict. The fear of eternal glory is a fundamental
human neurosis, and it is probably the definitive neurosis.

Even the mystics who are granted particular intimations of beatitude know a certain conflict; actually, the
temporary vision of Heaven can make temporal obscurantism all the more painful. "For we know that the
Law is spiritual; but I am carnal, sold under sin. For
that which I do I allow not; for what I would, that do
I not; but what I hate, that I do." (*Rom. 7:14-15*) This,
too, was Saint Augustine's distress: "I am caught up to
Thee by thy love only to be swept back by my own
weight . . ." With a certain resignation, even with a re-
signed good humor, the saints have sometimes felt, with-

out self-pity, like Dickensian waifs shivering in the snow as they gaze through a glazed window at a golden fire and a flaming pudding. The dark night outside the eternal warmth is, to be specific in mystical language, two dark nights. The first is the night of the senses, a melange of spiritual fatigues and discouragements known as malaise, ennui, accidie. The second and deeper dark is the night of the soul, a spiritual desolation capable of but one chant, the elegiac lament of Love's own bereftment: "Eli, Eli, Lama Sabacthani." But because they can be expressed, from whatever plaintive depths, the nights are such that they can precede a dawn of the integral personality. This is what Heaven on earth, or "realized eschatology" connotes.

Christ himself is the source for the progressive revelation of this reassuring wisdom: "Thy Kingdom come, Thy will be done on earth as it is in Heaven," (*Matt. 6:10; Luke 11:2*) "The Kingdom of God is come nigh unto you," (*Luke 10:9*) ". . . the Kingdom of God is within you." (*Luke 17:21*) Christ himself is the Kingdom, for that is the "Je suis l'état" of divine right. This is why the Second Vatican Council described Christ bringing the hymn of Heaven into our earthly exile. Prayer in all its forms participates in this song; when prayer becomes difficult and our souls feel arid, the soul needs to remember that prayer is not a dialogue with God but a duet. The formula of Saint Benedict was: *Sola quae cantat audit*: "Only [the soul] that sings really hears." Now the transforming effect of the Messianic song on sinners who confess their sins and become saints attests to the potency of divine harmony. As a certain pitch can break a glass, so a celestial pitch can tear the curtain between natural limitations and eternal life, and did so on Good Friday when the veil before the Holy of Holies was torn

open. In the earliest days of the experience, Saul of
Tarsus, ungainly, arrogant, grumpy and cruel, heard
the hymn on the Damascus road and completed his
earthly pilgrimage as an apostle of the eternal life he
had denied, the beauty he had vulgarized, the truth he
had twisted, the radiance he had tried to shred to tinsel.

As the early Fathers of the Church understood the
nature of man, human nature is capable of divinization,
or *theosis*, without lapsing into an indiscriminate panthe-
ism, and it becomes more divine by constant reference
to the eternal and other-worldly glory which is bestowed
on our insufficient condition by the Lord of Glory. The
Hebrew word for flesh has about it the suggestion of a
transparency; to live in the flesh is to live in "something
which shines forth." Whether we read Athanasius, Irenaeus, Cyril of Alexandria, or his lesser echo, Origen,
Gregory of Nyssa, or the two solemn Cappodocians,
Basil and Gregory of Nazianzen, the perception of man
as an ikon of Christ Glorified does not waver. It is a
refreshing adjustment to the diminished Heaven-consciousness of a secularized liberalism which has reduced
the spiritual life to a moralism redolent of the Stoics in
their quiet anger at misperceived creation. In the final
reckoning, the ability to sing the song of Heaven is the
singular and stable guarantee of true humanity. Emil
Brunner gave his account of it in *Man in Revolt*:

> God creates man in such a way that in this very cre-
> ation man is summoned to receive the Word actively,
> that is, he is called to listen, to understand, and to
> believe. God creates man's being in such a way that
> man knows that he is determined and conditioned by
> God, and in this fact is truly human. The being of
> man as an "I" is being from and in the Divine "Thou,"
> or, more exactly, from and in the Divine Word, whose
> claim "calls" man's being into existence . . .

The Divine Word is the perfect utterance which man cannot evade if he is to live, for he was created "over-against" the Word with a necessity to accept or reject it. And, says Brunner, that obligation by which man can fulfill or destroy God's purpose in creation is the distinguishing feature of human life. The hospitality of the Divine Word invites those intent on true humanity to enter their true home of Heaven, and this is perfect hospitality, far more than kindness or even friendship; it bears with it the "freedom of the guest," what the Dutch claim to mean when they call hospitality *gastyr-ijheid*. Only the perfect Host knows how to conquer loneliness without invading privacy or compromising dignity. Many reject Heaven because they think it means a public exposure, a communal indiscretion; and the hesitancy is betrayed in the jokes, which are only half-banter, about not wanting to ride around on clouds playing harps.

Pontius Pilate rejected the hospitality to preserve what he thought was the essential dignity of himself and his emperor, but only after acknowledging that he found no fault in the Host. For reasons he thought necessary, but which were absurd according to the divine economy, he chose to be *Frei aber einsam*, "Free but lonely." His example teaches the hard way that human freedom does not work properly through only empirical observation, but by trust in a deeper allusion. Authentic freedom is more than the possibility of choice, it is the possibility of the right choice. "The Kingdom of God comes not with observation: Neither shall they say, Lo here! or, lo there! for behold, the Kingdom of God is within you." (*Luke 17:20-21*) Just as faith seeks understanding, in Anselm's dictum, so also does the understanding need faith. So long as the intellect is not informed by faith, it will be anguished by the incontestable fact of Christ's faultlessness.

The most fertile imagination is utterly incapable of fabricating a faultless figure; the most offputting the defective characters in literary lore are those who were meant to be images of perfection, the witless gods of causes and races. But Christian eschatology lives by a sacramental consciousness which alone can unite intellect and faith in a comprehension of perfection apart from mythic polemicism. Jesus is not perfect because he proves a point; he is perfect because he is of Heaven. He cannot be a species of hero, because he is the reason for heroism. Mere heros of whatever stripe are not perfect enough to be lovable for eternity. Nothing less than Perfection is tolerable under the eternal circumstance. Marlowe's rhyming would be a mental torture after the first hundred years of it; Quintillian's most dulcet perorations would become a hideous shriek; Lincoln's quiet wood-whittling would be an intolerable scraping after time enough; and Penelope's weaving and unravelling would be a spiderish obsession soon enough; Florence Nightingale's nursing would turn into a plague for all time; even Thomas Jefferson would be tedious after a surfeit of declarations and palladian porches. But there cannot be too much Christ. Incontestably, there can be too much God-talk and it may even seem that people talk more about him than they talk with him; but even anti-Christians usually criticize Christians for not being Christian enough. The perpetual fascination of the historic consciousness with Jesus Christ is a singular reality in human experience, explicable only by the content of his absolute perfection.

Being an imperfect image of that perfection, but an image nonetheless, the soul is constantly drawn toward

it, not fatally as a fly to a web, but providentially. We
are not insects, nor is the shining mount of Transfiguration a trap. We are as human as Peter, James and John
who saw the perfect glory of Heaven transfigured before
them, perfect flesh manifest for the first time as that
"which shines forth." And we, like those three in their
unaided reason, make imperfect attempts to hallow the
encounter, unaware that the encounter is the hallower.
Then we are rather like Robert Browning writing in
Pippa Passes, "God's in his heaven / All's right with the
world," when the fact of the matter is that Heaven is in
God. Confused by the sight of Heaven pouring through
the flesh of a man, the three apostles wanted to build
several shrines, as though the two figures with Christ,
Moses and Elijah, were doing the same thing. They were
mistaken, but at least they wanted to anchor the radiance
in an allusion more portentous than native cleverness.
In the same fervor Jacob clutched his dreamy ladder,
and Plato imagined in symposium: "What if a man had
two eyes to see the true beauty, I mean pure and clear
and unalloyed, not clogged with the pollutions of morality and all the colors and vanities of human life, and
hold converse with the true beauty which is divine."

Redounding with the radiance of the Transfiguration,
the sacraments of the Church makes things holy because
they contain what they signify; and Christ obtains what
he signifies because he is the Holy. Reality is rooted in
this affirmation; and so we repeat the maxim that everything is either allusion or illusion. And consequently, all
that is truly human is allusory. A woman has had in her
the alphabet of converse with the true beauty since her
conception, and puts on perfume to breathe that flawless
scent behind every bloom and spice in creation. Likewise
a man as heir of glory shines his shoes because some

voice calls him to set them on silver stairs toward a gilded city. But the perfume and polish are preludes to scent and shine, like looking through tinted steam and rainbows to the home of the rose and the red of Mars, bottled and burnished lovelinesses which fade before the Enticer himself who is Love and the glory of Love: "Arise, shine; for thy light is come, and the glory of the Lord is risen upon thee." (*Isa. 60:1*) Scent will be seen as it now is smelled; light will be smelled as it now is seen. Intransitive verbs, like "to be" will become transitive and we shall be able to view existence, instead of just holding various views on it.

Visionary as this is, it is also historic; God told the father of our history, Abraham; "Walk in my sight and be perfect." (*Gen. 17:1*) What is this, then, but the announcement of the Beatific Vision which is possible for us by having been promised to our fathers. If the details of it are beyond appreciation, and even beyond normal appetite, it is because of a wonder too deep for natural astonishment. Natural sense should not want to breathe in the smell of light, nor should eyes strain to see the odor of sanctity. Moses would have been as disinterested before the event to know that he was about to encounter a burning bush that did not burn. Nor should we think that we might appreciate it more if we simply stretched the imagination. That might work with natural wonder; for instance, it takes much imagination to picture the atoms of a star being stripped from their nuclei by pressures of a hundred thousand trillion pounds per square inch. Things like that would seem to make the accounts of Heaven, the apocalyptic sight of crystal seas and wheels within wheels, positively unimaginative. And well they should, for they were not imagined but seen through the operation of the Holy Spirit. That is why

we have said that Heaven is not to be pictured, but
entered. We are dealing not with a mural but with a
window. To gaze upon God is more like inhaling than
looking, for we are in his image; and if the Beatific
Vision is a perplexing idea, it is so because we have never
seen sight.

The senses are necessarily limited in this natural life
so that we might not consume more than we are capable
of digesting. A glass of festive champagne can kill a baby,
and human nature still is in its spiritual infancy. Only
three children could not be destroyed by too much joy:
the Church celebrates most saints on the day each died
since it is the "heavenly birthday," but John the Baptist,
the Virgin Mary, and Jesus Christ are fêted on their
natural birthdays because those births helped to bring
Heaven to earth in a palpable way. Peculiar events sur-
rounded the births; that makes them more difficult to
understand, but Cardinal Newman said a thousand difficulties do not make one doubt.

A person who wants to believe in the larger life of
Heaven to come may be perplexed and guilty at what
seems to be insuperable difficulties about its existence.
These are, upon consideration, hardly doubts at all but
confusions about the tenacity of earth. This beguiling
and frightening planet has a commanding sway over our
better judgement, for at times we feel so contented that
we do not care to abandon it and at other times we feel
so insecure we do not dare move beyond it. The dilemma
cannot be resolved without first at least moving beyond
complacency and insecurity. Each is a form of fear and
"He who fears is not perfected in love." (*1 John 4:18*)
What we need, it may safely be said, is the kind of delight
in God *behind* creation that he has for us *in* creation, a
delight such as that he showed when he rejoiced in the

birds of the sky and the wild flowers of the field, and
then turned to us and said that we are of much more
value than they, even more valuable than the finery of
Solomon in all his glory. It would be very difficult indeed
to anticipate the Beatific Vision without considering this
delight; for while we wonder why or how we should
keep looking at God, at least one part of the wonder is
that God should be so happy to look at us. Saint Francis
de Sales said, "Do not fear God in the least, for he does
not want to do you harm; but love him greatly, because
he wants to do you great good."

In the garden wall of an English college there is a
small blue door which was familiar to Lewis Carroll. A
former Dean of the college liked to remind visitors of
its significance for Alice, and as he walked around it, his
craggy frame and blunt demeanor took on a positive
whimsicality. Many who were awed by his combination
of clerical dignity and nautical vocabulary would agree
that he towered most loftily each time he knelt on his
gaitered decanal knees to fiddle with the old keyhole,
as onlookers dawdled with their martini olives and cuc-
umber sandwiches. Some few years later, this writer
stood at his grave in the cathedral shadow on the other
side of the wall; ponderous eschatology aside, it was
damnably irrefutable, as he might have put it, that Cuth-
bert had gotten through the door. Narrow indeed is the
way that leads to salvation, but narrowmindedness does
not open it, only wanderlust: "I am the door: If any man
enter in by me, he shall be saved, and shall go in and
out and find pasture." (*1 Cor. 13:12*) The youngest bib-
liophile knows that Alice made it through both the door
and the looking glass because they are not at all that
different. In fact and not in fiction, in the instance of
Heaven where figures of speech are the only species of

speech that does figure up, the door and the looking glass are quite the same: "For now we see through a mirror darkly: but then face to face; now I know in part, but then I shall know even as I am known." (*1 Cor. 13:12*) And we shall get in. The whole world and all meaning hangs on that. We shall get in, for we have it on the confidence of the only man who never lied. He said that if it were not so, he would have told us (*John 14:2*).

To know a thing as we are known is a nearly impossible speculation, admitting as it does, as often as we hesitate to admit it, that there is a mind which knows the human nature better than humans know themselves. Here is the triple acquaintance with us of our Creator and of our Savior and of our Sanctifier. The myriad blessed souls in Heaven finally perceive their reality solely by seeing this Holy Trinity and so, in the words of Thomas à Kempis, they "fly, run and rejoice." Of this reasonably unimaginable transport, in which the human creature beholds the divine essence without the aid of any medium or reflection or process of reasoning, Pope Benedict XII wrote in the constitution *Benedictus Deus* in 1336:

> We define that, since the passion and death of the Lord Jesus Christ, (the souls in Heaven) have seen and do see the divine essence with an intuitive and even face-to-face vision, without interposition of any creature in the function of the object seen. Rather, the divine essence immediately manifests itself to them plainly, clearly, openly.

> We also define that those who see the divine essence in this way receive great joy from it, and that because of this vision and enjoyment the souls of those who have already died are truly blessed and possess life and eternal rest.

> We further define that the souls of those who die
> hereafter will see the same divine essence and will
> enjoy it before the general judgement.
>
> We define that this vision of the divine essence and
> the enjoyment of it do away with the acts of faith and
> hope of those souls, insofar as faith and hope are
> theological virtues in the proper sense.
>
> And we define that after this intuitive and face-to-
> face vision has or will have begun for these souls, the
> same vision and enjoyment remains continuously
> without any interruption or abolition of the vision and
> enjoyment and will remain up till the final judgement
> and from then on forever.

One Twentieth Century choirboy, oblivious to those
ancient words, used to while away the long moments of
the sermon by studying a large stained glass window on
the opposite wall, on the preacher's left. To the boy's
critical eye it was a mighty work of art, combining, not
altogether accurately, (although he was not familiar with
them at the time), the languid lines of Tiffany and Ro-
setti, through a faint mother-of-pearl haze, where a
good number of men and women in loungewear seemed
to be gracefully gliding around an alabaster hall which
looked like the Palm Court in the Plaza Hotel. If Heaven
is got at more through windows than through pictures,
it is very satisfactory to put the picture on the window;
at least this picture saved the boy ever after from thinking that Heaven is full of dead people. Now that he has
grown he is more grateful to glaziers and artists than to
some catechists and theologians. He is grateful indeed
to popes who define the truth, but for that he is not
thankless toward painters who assume that joy might
also be enjoyable.

He is also more indebted to them than to some teachers who dismiss the practical applications of Heaven as anthropomorphic. It would be repulsive for an anthropoid not to be anthropomorphic. From what the most sensible people have shown over the years, the endless contemplation of God will amplify individual distinctiveness. The baseball fan will not be alien to it, nor will those who long for rainy afternoons and the chance at last to read Thackeray. For metaphors of this social joy, men and women in bathrobes eating chocolate eclairs in marble halls are certainly no less adequate than the mirage of a world benignly administered by social democrats. If any better symbol should be asked for, you might settle for Dante's moving River of Light and the motionless white Rose. Like Saint John in vision of glassy gold and pearl, so Dante realized in his closing verses that Heaven is too mysterious to be complex, and that when the secret of the Empyrean is encountered, one will face the One. In the fourteenth century, Ruysbroeck wrote in *De Calculo*:

> When love has carried us above and beyond all things, above the light, into the Divine Dark, there we are wrought and transformed by the Eternal Word Who is the image of the Father; and as the air is penetrated by the sun, there we receive in idleness of spirit the Incomprehensible Light, enfolding us and penetrating us. And this Light is nothing else but an infinite gazing and seeing. We behold that which we are, and we are that which we behold; because our thought, life and being are uplifted in simplicity and made one with the Truth which is God.

It becomes appreciable in the most unexpected moments: Elizabeth Ann Seton taking the hand of her dying husband under quarantine and in a strange land, a bedridden priest trying to raise his chalice for the last time, tourists hearing the ancient bells in their ancestral towns. These are not the moments which add up to hours; they are more the incalculable minutiae of eternity, and indicate that this length of life is as short as it is long, an up-and-down kind of time instead of the back-and-forth kind we can compute. The Jews knew this as they carried the baggage of their historic chosenness up the long stairs of their high Temple: "I was glad when they said unto me, We will go into the house of the Lord. Our feet shall stand in thy gates O Jerusalem." (*Psalm 122:1-2*) The singers did not entirely foresee how horizontal time would cross vertical time just beyond those gates, on a hill shaped like a skull, and by so doing would open the gates to a new Jerusalem.

Beginning and end, up and down, dawn and sunset, catharsis and transfiguration, incarnation and ascension are united, and much is going on that we cannot see. But there was one like us who saw much; he had no more grace available to him than we have, but he accepted it and used it better: "I John saw the holy city . . ." (*Rev. 21:2*) It is home to the temper of the universe, and provides four welcomes just as Hippocrates quartered human nature into temperaments.

Entering by the eastern gates of the new City is a young crowd, and impulsive: David and Joan and Therese, and the soldiers who were flung against guns before aged hands had taken up peace pens; the fresh and eager who did not outlive the springtime taste of beauty and truth and goodness; the vigorous who broke records and whose deaths broke hearts.

Through the southern way pour the phlegmatic souls who spent half their lives basking almost as if by neglect, polishing jade and poaching lobsters, taking up gaudy colors and vows, and the other half of their time laughing at their own bravado. These are the asymmetrical and non-Euclidean types who sing to the sky instead of taking its temperature, wondering why the rest of the world is not ruddy and wine-glad.

The gates of the north open to the choleric and analytical ones, who with a tweedy officiousness smoked pipes and cured obscure diseases, built bridges that do not collapse, and at predictable intervals lost faith in God who is not as circumspect as they.

There is a west, no doubt about it. There never was an east without one. Through its gates passes a slower procession, longer all the while and wistful at the end. Each in it is laden with good wishes and kindly memories and grandchildren and dented trophies and some of the old furniture and ragged lace the young overlooked in their rush. The sun is behind them and you cannot see the wrinkles on their faces anymore.

The light is not dying, and it gets brighter the deeper the sun sinks into dust, and brightest when the sun disappears with no moon to catch its dregs. The light, if you will, is shining in the dark, intolerably so to natural vision designed to adjust by day and night, and awesomely so to those about to walk into the center of it. The darkness does not overcome the tint and tone. Some of the crowd entering the gates are amazed to find it there; and some are blankly astonished to find themselves there; and some are confused to see what was supposed to be an ephemeral self-projection; and some are annoyed to find the others there. But they are agreed on one truth: in the middle of the City is a lamb and the lamb is also a man and the man is also a god.

In differing degrees, or as the Council of Florence said it, "some more perfectly than others according to their respective merits," they move closer to the center which, without striving wind or fanfare, occupies everywhere. They know immediately and without mental exploration that the lamb is Lamb, the man is Man, and the god is, in blatant response to the ceaseless petitions of will and conscience, God. How long from here it is in space or time is not the point, and is quite irrelevant.

When Saint Thomas More was told that he might enjoy his fair house at Chelsea with its library and gallery and garden and merry company for perhaps twenty years more, if he would compromise obedience to truth, he said it would be a bad calculation that for the sake of a hundred or even a thousand years he would risk the loss of eternity. The only point, and the one good calculation, is that the heart has a universe and the universe a heart. The heart is not heavenly at all. It is Heaven. "If it were not so I would have told you."

Jerusalem the golden, With milk and honey blest,
Beneath thy contemplation Sink heart and voice op-
  prest:
I know not, O I know not, What joys await us there;
What radiancy of glory, What bliss beyond compare!

They stand, those halls of Sion, All jubilant with song,
And bright with many an angel, And all the martyr
  throng:
The Prince is ever in them, The daylight is serene;
The pastures of the blessed Are decked in glorious
  sheen.

There is the throne of David; And there from care
  released,
The shout of them that triumph, The song of them
  that feast;
And they who with their Leader Have conquered in
  the fight,
For ever and for ever Are clad in robes of white.

O sweet and blessed country, The Home of God's
     elect!
O sweet and blessed country That eager hearts expect!
Jesus, in mercy bring us To that dear land of rest,
Who art, with God the Father, And Spirit ever blest.

                        Saint Bernard of Cluny, c. 1145